The American Motorcycle Girls

1900 to 1950

Motorcyclist

20¢ THE COPY · DOLLAR AND A QUARTER THE YEAR

JUNE NINETEEN FORTY

The American Motorcycle Girls

1900 to 1950

A Photographic History of Early Women Motorcyclists

Cristine Sommer Simmons

Author/publisher of best-selling *Patrick Wants to Ride*. Co-founder of *Harley Women*
Honorary Lifetime Member of Women in the Wind
2003 Inductee of the National Motorcycle Hall of Fame, Anamosa, Iowa
2003 Inductee of the American Motorcycle Association Hall of Fame, Pickerington, Ohio
2008 Inductee of the Sturgis Motorcycle Hall of Fame, Sturgis, South Dakota

Foreword by Karen Davidson

Great-granddaughter of Harley-Davidson co-founder William A. Davidson
1991 Council of Fashion Designers of America special award winner
Creative Director, General Merchandise, Harley-Davidson Motor Company

PARKER
HOUSE

Parker House Publishing Inc.
1826 Tower Drive
Stillwater, Minnesota 55082, USA
www.parkerhousepublishing.com

ISBN-13: 978-0-9817270-5-9

Cover and book design: Chris Fayers
Editor: Kathleen Donohue
Index: Kristal Leebrick
Front cover photo of Dot Smith, courtesy A.M.A. Archives
Back cover photo of Cris Sommer Simmons, courtesy Michael Lichter
Half-title photo of Hazel Bilty, courtesy Harley-Davidson Archives, copright H-D
Opposite the title page, courtesy *Motorcyclist* magazine
This spread photo, Fair Riders, Hokokus, New Jersey, courtesy Simmons Family Collection

Manufactured in China by World Print Limited, Kowloon, Hong Kong

10 9 8 7 6 5 4 3 2 1

PARKER
HOUSE

Contents

Foreword by Karen Davidson
6

An introduction to Cristine Sommer Simmons
8

Acknowledgments
10

An introduction to *The American Motorcycle Girls*
12

1900 to 1912
16

1913 to 1919
48

1920 to 1929
110

1930 to 1939
156

1940 to 1949
192

1950
232

Index
240

Foreword
by Karen Davidson

We've got it good today. We've got paved roads. And we've got motorcycles that ride for tens of thousands of miles on those smooth roads without a problem. We've got high performance gear, from helmets to boots that specifically outfit all kinds of women for all kinds of weather and all kinds of riding. And we have fully equipped service stations, cell phones, GPS, and a multitude of choices for a place to eat and stay the night in comfort.

Consider the woman of the early days of motorcycling some 100 years ago. Pioneer. Individualist. Adventurer. From the comfort of our time we can savor an antique motorcycle for its nostalgic beauty. But think of what it was to ride without all that we have now. The roads were rough and maps were most likely either incomplete or worse, non-existent. Motorcycles weren't the technological machines they've become as a result of today's incredible advances in design, testing and engineering. Of course those early machines were ridden long distances, but it certainly wasn't as often a flawless a trip as it is today. And if you were to break down, you had to manage without 24-hour roadside service, without the motel just down the road. It's hard to imagine that any rain gear worked as well as our choices today. The landscape wasn't dotted with restaurants and service stations to pull into conveniently. Perhaps unsurprisingly our visit to the dealer today is more likely for pleasure than it is to replace the inner tube in a tire for the third time that day.

Women also have the right to vote today, and so much more. Beyond the bikes, the roads, the gear, and the amenities of travel, consider the perceived "place" of women in society in the early 20th century. Now think of those women who bucked the confinement of the then society's definition of them and rode motorcycles. Let's just put it this way, rebels on motorcycles aren't limited to male stereotypes born in movies of the 1950s. Enough said.

Today the words "vacation" and "adventure" are seemingly interchangeable. I'd guess that the women who pioneered motorcycling wouldn't confuse the two. And as much as there is a tradition toward the adventure in motorcycling, there is also the tradition of sharing stories.

As many riders will attest to, the motorcycle makes road travel experiences much more intimate. Often riders recount their personal connection to their bike. Their bike becomes a partner on the journey, the conduit that bridges guts and accomplishment.

The stories you are about to read are the true stories of guts, glory and a deep-seated love for adventure of women who pursued their dreams as motorcyclists. They epitomize the very existence of a strong-willed group of female motorcyclists, awash with conviction, who achieved many "firsts". All at a time in our history (from 1900 to 1950) when there were many pioneers in a multitude of other fields making firsts happen throughout America.

They include the first woman to ride a complete circuit of the U.S.A. on a motorcycle, the first woman to ride icy roads to the summit of Pikes Peak in -10° F on a motorcycle, and the first mother/daughter duo to cross the U.S. on a motorcycle.

These pioneering women motorcyclists and their stories of their trials, tribulations, rule busting, and occasional law breaking antics inspire us today as they did back 50 or even 100 years ago.

We've got it good. We have beautiful bikes, gorgeous roads and high tech gear, all making it more likely we'll have a great adventure on our bikes. And we're lucky to have these women who set the pace and whose stories are here to inspire us. Thanks to Cris Sommer Simmons' diligence and vision to take on the role of storyteller and archivist. She brings us these stories and pictures of the first women motorcyclists who embraced motorcycling as their sport of choice, knowing that it is indeed about the journey, the quest for adventure and a wild ride.

Karen Davidson has a strong natural instinct about the mystique of Harley-Davidson from a lifetime of living the Harley-Davidson experience. Karen is the great-granddaughter of the company's co-founder, William A. Davidson, and has been riding motorcycles since she was nine.

Karen joined Harley-Davidson Motor Company in 1989 helping co-create a new, branded line of apparel and accessories for its customers—Harley-Davidson MotorClothes. Today, Karen is the Director of Creative for General Merchandise.

Biography from the Harley-Davidson web site 2009 with permission

Daytona 2009. *Harley-Davidson Archives, copyright H-D*

An Introduction to
Cristine Sommer Simmons

In the historically male-dominated world of motorcycling, no one has more passion for motorcycles than Cris. She has enjoyed a lifetime love affair with two wheels. An eager passenger on her stepfather's motorcycle by age nine, she remembers studying how to shift so that she could one day ride on her own. Cris rode her first motorcycle solo at fourteen, learning in the parking lot of the local Wonder Bread Outlet Store. She convinced her mother and stepfather to help her buy her first bike—a Yamaha Twin Jet 100cc. Word spread like wildfire about the neighborhood "girl rider" with the fast bike. Cris got her first Harley at nineteen, and has never looked back.

Cris was a longtime member of the Women's International Motorcycle Association and in 1984, co-founded the second chapter of Women in the Wind. A year later she co-founded the world's first motorcycle magazine for women motorcyclists called *Harley Women*. For over five years, she acted as co-publisher and editor, often riding her motorcycle across the country to find the stories. On one such ride in 1989 she met her husband-to-be, rocker and fellow motorcycle enthusiast, Doobie Brothers band member Patrick Simmons.

For several years in the late 1980s, Cris appeared in countless national newspaper articles, radio and television talk shows as a representative and advocate of the growing number of women who rode on the front of their own motorcycles. In 1988, she was awarded an Honorary Lifetime membership to Women in the Wind. Cris is a twenty-three year A.M.A. member, lifetime H.O.G. member and a Motor Maid. In 1990, she was honored as a pioneering woman motorcyclist in the American Motorcycle Association's Women in Motorcycling exhibit in the A.M.A.'s museum at Westerville, Ohio.

After selling her interest in *Harley Women*, Cris began a fifteen-year stint as a freelance motorcycle journalist, writing extensively for many magazines in the U.S.A., including *American Iron, Motorcycle Collector, Iron Works, Easyriders,* and *V-Twin*, as well as magazines in Japan, Spain and in Australia. Cris also penned her own column for over twelve years in the popular Japanese Harley magazine, *Hot Bike Japan*.

In 1994, Cris wrote and self-published the award-winning children's book *Patrick Wants to Ride*, for which she was honored with the A.M.A.'s Brighter Image MVP Award. Now in its third printing, the book has sold over 12,000 copies. Cris has also co-written a screenplay about women motorcyclists.

In 1995, Cris was one of four women featured in *Biker Women,* an original documentary for Turner Broadcasting. This well-received show set viewing records.

In 2003, Cris was proud to be inducted into the National Motorcycle Hall of Fame and the American Motorcycle Heritage Foundation Motorcycle Hall of Fame. In 2008, she was inducted into the Sturgis Motorcycle Hall of Fame in South Dakota.

She currently rides a 1988 Harley-Davidson Heritage and a 1934 Harley-Davidson VLD. She lives in Maui, Hawaii with her husband Pat and their three children, Lindsey, Josh and Patrick.

Michael Lichter

Acknowledgements

I would like to thank the following people—without whom this book would not have been possible—for digging into their collections and old shoeboxes to share their wonderful photographs and family stories with me.

Many thanks to Mark Allen, Jackie Atkins, Ken Beal, Darris Blackford and Patty Humphries of A. D. Farrow Co. To Jeff Carstensen and John Parham from the National Motorcycle Museum, Anamosa, Iowa, Steve Cornish, Craig Dove, Carl Edeburn, Don Emde, Jane Farrow Langley, Walt Greenwood, Jerry Hooker of www. motorcyclememories.com.

Thanks to Paul Jamiol, Paul Joyce, Ken Magri, Pepper Massey, the late Samantha Morgan, the *Chrome Cowgirl*—Sasha Mullins, Jack Nagengast, Kay Nerland, OnlyClassics, the Pelaquin family, and Virginia Richardson. To the family of Dot Robinson, Betty Fauls Robinson and Ron Rae. To Marilyn Slater, Dal Smilie, Sandy Steiner, Robert Van Buren, the family of Clara Wagner, daughters Dorothy Sippy and Lucy Dettmer. To the Walker family, Dale and Matt Walksler of the Wheels Through Time Museum, Bill Wills, and Geert Versleyen of www.yesterdays.nl.

Thanks to the Harley-Davidson Motor Company for permission to publish photographs from their archives.

The Davidson family has always been an inspiration. Willie G. and Nancy, Bill and Michael, thanks for keeping the dream alive. Karen, you are a sister rider and I am proud to have you write the Foreword for this book. Thank you so much.

Thanks to Steve Wright for his wonderful books on the subject of antique motorcycles and the people who rode them, which inspired me from the first time I saw one over twenty years ago.

Thanks to Ruth "Sis" Baer Arnold and the Baer family: Butch, Tom and Tim for sharing their stories and photos. Also to Ruth's son Bob Arnold for helping to fill in the blanks.

Special thanks to Maggie Humberston, my new friend and Head of Library and Archives from the Museum of Springfield History, Springfield, Massachusetts, for the almost daily emails and permission to publish some of the beautiful photos from the Esta Mathos Indian Motorcycle Collection.

I am indebted to the American Motorcycle Association: Mark Mederski , Grant Parsons and Tapitha Davis for all the time and energy answering my long winded emails.

Thanks to Mitch Boehm and *Motorcyclist* magazine for multiple photographs. And thanks to Mike FitzSimons for identifying our "mystery bike".

Special thanks to my publisher Tim Parker, of Parker House Publishing, for sharing my vision and helping to bring this dream to life. You are a joy to work with.

It was a pleasure to work with our talented copy editor Kathleen Donohue. She helped to brighten my rough edges and understood my voice.

Thanks to Michael Lichter for the photo used on page nine and the back cover and for the twenty-three years of friendship; and Steve Temple who works with Michael.

I would like to thank Patti Carpenter for her support, kindness and help in blazing the trail for the rest of us female motorcycle journalists.

To former Wall of Death rider, Cookie Crum, thanks for the phone calls, the friendship and the exciting explanation of how to actually ride the Wall of Death.

A big thank you to the amazing Gloria Tramontin Struck, another new friend, who is still riding and dreaming and whose optimism and zest for life continues to inspire me.

I'm extremely grateful to Margaret Wilson for the all she has done to help promote women motorcyclists through all the years. Thank you Margaret!

I am indebted to my Motor Maid sisters for keeping the flame alive. Thank you for trusting me with the photos of those who came before us. I am proud to honor them in this book. Special thanks to President Brenda Thatcher and Historian Kathy Disney.

Thanks to Tanner Watt, for creative encouragement, computer questions and helping me get started all those months ago in my kitchen.

A BIG shout out to my "girls". To best friend Gail DeMarco, thanks for making me smile and laugh when I didn't always feel like it and for inspiring me with your photography. Nicole Sepulveda, a special thanks for your help and expertise with all those scans and for coming to my rescue in the heat of my deadline. (See. . . all nighters CAN be fun. . . who needs sleep?) Thanks to my Maui Girls, the "other" Gail, Gail Swanson and Amy Holland McDonald for being the best friends a girl could ever ask for.

Thanks to my friends Willie Nelson and Mike McDonald for the kind words and for endorsing my book. Your encouragement has meant a lot. If you ever need my help in writing a song, let me know.

Very special thanks to my extremely sweet and kind husband Pat, my own personal, "in-house", motorcycle collector/historian extraordinaire, who encouraged and loved me every step of the way. He tirelessly answered my never-ending string of questions about old bikes at all hours of the night (especially when he was trying to sleep), and held up the fort brilliantly when I was too busy. I love you.

To my kids, whom I am so proud of, daughter and friend, Lindsey, for your love, daily insight and editing skills. To my sons, Josh and Pat, see. . . other moms rode motorcycles too! Thanks for understanding me. I love you and am so proud of both of you.

Thanks to my mom, Shirlee, a great writer herself who started it all by actually letting me have a motorcycle. She also gave me the writing gene and the spark to try. To my dad Joe, for the "thrill" gene and letting me fly his airplane with him as a young girl. To my beautiful sister Rachel and my great brothers, Tim, Mark, Joe, Rick and Jason for sticking together through it all. I love all of you guys! Yes. . . folks, sisters CAN teach their brothers how to ride motorcycles (yes, even you Rick! Though I won't let you ride mine again).

Special thanks and unending gratitude to all the women who appear in this book and who paved the way for the rest of us. I feel lucky to be able to tell your stories and only hope I can do you justice.

In loving memory of Fran Crane, Marla Garber, Olive Hager, Samantha Morgan and my friend Louise Scherbyn.

An Introduction to
The American
Motorcycle Girls
1900 to 1950

As the saying goes, before one can run, one must learn to walk. Just as naturally, before women dared to ride motorcycles, there were the first women bicyclists. For the so-called "gentler sex", the fashionable era of bicycle riding began in America in 1894, inspired by a doctor's wife who had first learned to ride a bicycle on the streets of Paris. Her friends and family must have been horrified at the thought of her riding such a contraption. In spite of the opposition, she and her bicycle appeared on the boulevard regularly, gliding effortlessly along, her enjoyment so obvious and infectious that others wanted to ride as well.

By the following year, the bicycling craze hit New York with a wave of enthusiasm that overwhelmed the city. Riding schools were filled with aspiring cyclists from morning 'til night, and all day long on the boulevard cyclists cruised up and down in neat parallel lines. Horses quickly diminished in significance—the saddle paths in Central Park were nearly deserted. Bicycle shops sprang up along the most popular routes of travel almost overnight. Between 1897 and 1898, the bicycle furor reached its highest pitch. When women joined this pedal parade, it was more than an exciting new amusement; it was the beginning of something very significant, and the catalyst of more changes to come.

For women, riding bicycles (and soon motorcycles) precipitated another first— the earliest appearance of the short skirt. Far from the fancy of fashion, this was a matter of necessity—a long skirt fell dangerously close to the rear wheel, a threat to life and limb. It could get caught up in the chain or the wheel, and a soaking wet skirt on rainy days was even worse. From such bondage the wheel delivered the girl of 1900.

While much of the early history of women in motorcycling is elusive, we *do* know that they were active participants by the turn of the century. In Europe, women were already quite active in this thrilling new sport. Certainly, many women would have found motorcycling as exhilarating as their male counterparts did. How could they not? Already riding bicycles, they knew the thrill of the wind in their faces. By all available evidence, American women seem to have been riding motorcycles about as long as men. Scores of photos show them enjoying the early days of motorcycling right alongside their male counterparts. Surely, in the earliest of days, motorcycles were noisy, oil-splattering contraptions, and the men who dared to ride them were often thought

of as dirty ruffians. A few years of refinement resulted in a cleaner ride—and soon, motorcycles were as desirable a vehicle as an automobile. One could ride all day long in a light suit and arrive at one's destination, none the worse for wear, with only a bit of dust to brush off from the day's trip. Just one more reason women were drawn to motorcycling. They weren't about to be left out of the exhilaration of riding—especially when they didn't have to get dirty to do it! Once a woman mastered the technique of handling a motorcycle, that was all it took. She was off!

Though there were most likely others who braved the unknown before her, one of the earliest known American woman to conquer riding a motorcycle in 1902 was Mrs. G.N. Rogers from Schenectady, New York. The young lady amazed everyone, men and women, with her natural ability, but to her, it was just an "interesting" thing to do.

Dorothy Rice was the well-heeled daughter of New York millionaire and renowned chess master Isaac Rice. In 1906, Dorothy was hailed as one of the first girls to ride a motorcycle in America—and the first in New York City. Understandably, Mr. Rice was not in favor of his debutante daughter riding such a machine. Hoping to scare some sense into the young lady, when she happened to be visiting away from home, he sent a sobering story clipped from the newspaper reporting a fatal motorcycle accident. By the next mail, a letter came back with another clipping. The headline read: "Man Dies in Theatre." With it, Dorothy enclosed a note; "Do you intend to keep me from going to the theatre because a man once died there?" Her father soon gave in, and Dorothy got her first motorcycle at the tender age of sixteen.

Dorothy and her brother became a common sight, riding their blue motorcycles up Riverside Drive. When patrolmen of the newly created Cycle Squad of the New York Police Department heard that Miss Rice would be traveling abroad for several years, they breathed a sigh of relief—and promptly began to reminisce about her daring work on the motorcycle through the streets of New York, and the many fruitless chases she had inspired. "Miss Rice was the most daring motorcyclist in this city", said one policeman, with grudging admiration. "She used to leave her home on Riverside Drive and race up the drive … at a clip that simply distanced us."

Dorothy was a beautiful contradiction—a debutante who scorned society. Headline writers called her "The Blue Streak Girl" for her occasional arrests, speeding through Manhattan on her blue motorcycle. In 1908, she got a ticket for going eighteen mph on Fifth Avenue. The fine? A very steep ten dollars.

In November of 1909, Dorothy attended the Sunday afternoon races at the Guttenburg Track in New Jersey. Dorothy wanted to compete in the five-mile race, but was not permitted to ride; regulations strictly forbade it, especially in competition against men. In anticipation of Dorothy's expected flouting of the rules, riders were given this stern warning: any rider who loaned Dorothy Rice a machine would be suspended for a year. But before the proclamation-issuing judge arrived at the track to stop her, Miss Rice had already ridden a trial mile in a stunning time—one minute, thirteen seconds.

There are no existing records as to exactly how many women motorcyclists there were in America during the early years of motorcycling. But by 1913, it was estimated that there were over 500 in England.

While surely women were discovering the motorcycle in other parts of America, New York was clearly an exciting place to be, and the press thrilled to cover the exploits of these daring motorcycle girls:

> "Half a dozen young women living on Riverside Drive have
> abandoned the bridal path for the motorcycle, and every morning they

may be seen flying north along Broadway into Westchester county, and on through Yonkers to the exclusive Ardsley Club. The weather has been favorable for these trips, and the roads are ideal for fast riding."
—*Motorcycle Illustrated*, May, 1908

Women weren't just riding around town either. In 1908, two adventurous young women from Syracuse, New York, Sophie Wardwell and Betty Wenbourne, planned a month's journey from Syracuse, to Kansas City. While their families were probably not as pleased with the plan, the women were confident that their experience, both on motorcycles and on previous long trips, would see them safely through. Sophie and Betty were certain they could make the complete trip in one month—and that they did.

New York wasn't the only state filled with adventurous females. Massachusetts women were also enthusiastically taking up the sport:

"Mrs. Henry W. Robinson, of Waltham, MA is one of the few women riders in the Bay State. She is familiar with every part of nearly all the various makes and for some years has spent much of her time at her husband's motorcycle agency and repair shop on Crescent Street, directly under the rooms occupied by the Waltham Motorcycle Club. She can repair a machine or fix a tire as easily as her husband and never yet has been obligated to walk home after a breakdown."
—*Motorcycle Illustrated*, May 15, 1909

Popularity of the motorcycle for transportation soared between 1910 and 1915: the motorcycle industry really took off. In 1912 and 1913, more than sixty new brands were introduced. Within a few short years, women like the audacious mother and daughter duo, Effie and Avis Hotchkiss, were riding across the country. While most mothers were helping their daughters learn piano or plan their weddings, Effie and Avis set a record for the first transcontinental sidecar crossing by women in 1915. In 1916, the equally adventurous Van Buren sisters, Adeline and Augusta, piloted their 1916 Indian Power Plus motorcycles from New York to California, becoming the first women to ride across the country on solo motorcycles.

Women weren't just riding motorcycles—they were riding fast—often faster than men. In 1911, Viola Culip and Mabel Masters, sixteen-year-old daughters from two of the wealthiest families in Indianapolis, became the first female motorcyclists to enter the racing business in Indiana. The pair rode to glory at the Middletown Fair and the State Fair in Indianapolis.

Out west in Denver, things were heating up as well:

"Plans are being perfected in this city for a brand new motorcycle club and the organization will be made up entirely of lady riders. Mrs. V.M. Vanderhoof, wife of "Doc" Vanderhoof, Indian and Excelsior subagent here, is at the head of the movement. Mrs. Van is one of the best lady motorcyclists in the country and she is a firm believer in the fact that the power two-wheeler is just as much a lady's machine as a man's.

'There is no reason in the world why a girl shouldn't ride a motorcycle just the same as she drives an automobile,' said Mrs. Vanderhoof in speaking of the proposed club. 'Operating a motorcycle is just as easy, if not easier, than driving a car and it is not any more dangerous. I believe a girl's motorcycle club would be a mighty good thing for Denver and I see no reason why it won't be a success. I already have ten girls lined up who are ready to form a club and I have only been on the job a few days. The boys ruled us out of the endurance run held here recently and so we're going to form a club of our own and hold our own endurance runs and other sports of like nature, with the motorcycle playing the leading role. The boys will have to take a back seat when we get going, too, or I'll miss my guess. We'll show them how a club ought to be run.'"

—*MotorCycling and Bicycling*, April 16, 1919

In the 1920s, the post WWI economy made automobiles more affordable—consequently, many motorcycle manufactures were forced out of business. The boom of the earlier decades was over. Cars flooded the roads. But when the stock market crash of 1929 brought prosperity to an end, for most, automobiles once again became unattainable. The motorcycle, a cheaper form of transportation, experienced a surge in popularity.

In the twenties, daredevil women like Olive Hager and Marjorie Kemp were headlining their own traveling carnival acts featuring the "Wall of Death". In these shows, Olive and Marjorie defied gravity, riding at high speeds on a perpendicular wall, thrilling audiences all over the country.

In the 1930s, the number of women motorcyclists soared. And once again, war changed lives. Between 1939 and 1945, women motorcyclists gave their all to help with the war effort. Dot Robinson, Theresa Wallach and "Gyp" Baker were just a few of the scores of women who risked their lives as motorcycle couriers for the military. Women also bravely escorted convoys and acted as dispatch riders. Afterwards, in the era of post-war prosperity, motorcycle riding evolved into more of a social activity. Local motorcycle club events were popular on weekends, attracting increasing numbers of men and women.

More and more women were discovering the independence and freedom the motorcycle offered. Like any other sport, the camaraderie of like-minded hobbyists grew right along with it. In 1938, the Sacramento Cyclettes, an all-girl motorcycle club, was formed. The most famous women's motorcycle club, the Motor Maids, was formed in 1940 with fifty-one women riders—and the club is still going strong today. The dream of long-time rider, Linda Dugeau, the club was a way for women to meet and support each other, and to share their love of motorcycles and the sense of freedom it brought them.

Many of the better-known women riders of that time were also Motor Maids. Dot Robinson was probably the most famous of any woman motorcyclist to this day; often called Motorcycling's First Lady, Dot was the first president of the club. Vera Griffin and Louise Scherbyn were very active members—Louise was also a well-known long distance and stunt rider who started the first all-girl motorcycle show in Waterloo, New York in 1940.

It's amazing to read about the awe-inspiring exploits of renowned women riders such as the fearless Dot Robinson and the extraordinary, courageous, cross-country riding Van Buren sisters … but these are just some of the stories. There are many unsung heroines whose stories we'll never know. If we're lucky, we may see a picture, hear a name, or read a short caption that tells just part of the tale. To see their smiles and sheer delight, faces in the wind … that's what this book is all about. If not for this book many of these images would remain unknown, uncelebrated. This book is dedicated to all of the heroic women who paved the way for the rest of us … with much gratitude.

1900 to 1912

OPPOSITE: Early Bicyclists *Circa 1905*
Simmons Family Collection

Bicycle Ladies *Circa 1900*
Taken in Cincinnati, Ohio around the turn of the century, these two fashionably dressed young women look ready for a ride right down to the ribbons on their handlebars.

Simmons Family Collection

Margaret Gast *1900*

Born in a small Bavarian town, Margaret Gast (Nagengast) emigrated from Germany to the United States at age sixteen. A robust, athletic girl, Margaret was persuaded by family and friends to take up bicycling. She became so adept at the sport that she entered the women's championship races, held at Long Island. When the officials couldn't see the point of allowing 'a mere child' to stand the strenuous competition, the resourceful Margaret made herself a few years older. She overwhelmed the competition.

In 1901 Margaret set a National Record for continuous riding—she covered 2,600 miles in twelve days, eight hours and fifty-five minutes—more than 200 miles a day. She would have pushed for 3,000 but regulations stated that no endurance rider should ride more than twelve hours out of twenty-four. Margaret had been riding for sixteen hours a day.

That same year, following the rules set by the Century Road Club, Margaret set a record for riding 2,000 miles, pedaling the distance in 222 hours and five and a half minutes. This broke the old record by three hours—a record set by a man. Margaret's record would remain unbroken until 1959.

It was just a matter of time before Margaret held all the women's records, and even broke a few of the men's. In 1905 she defeated Will Brown, a high-ranking professional male rider. She later turned pro as well, touring the American West and Canada with her own troupe of dare-devil riders. She performed exhibitions on bicycles, motorcycles and automobiles on perpendicular tracks, becoming the first woman to ride a motorcycle on a board track (motordrome) in competition. Margaret was also one of the first women of the so-called *weaker sex* to ride the perilous assent of the perpendicular wall of death. In this hazardous work Margaret often suffered injuries.

Margaret's machine of choice was the 1910 Flying Merkel. As many riders were, Margaret was an adept mechanic, and could—and often did—take her motorcycle apart and put it back together.

In 1913, still the National Women's Endurance Bicycle Rider Champion, Margaret proposed to point her bicycle toward Washington D.C. and ride with a banner draped across her handlebars that read, *Votes for Women*. She hoped to get through the Maryland mud in time to appear with the New York state delegation in their Women's Suffrage Parade in the nation's capitol.

After winning many honors, Margaret gave up racing and became a respected Manhattan massage therapist and physical trainer. Many of her clients were well-known celebrities of society and the stage. Margaret lived a full, exhilarating life until her death at age ninety-two.

Margaret on the Track

Circa 1910
Taken in Montreal, Canada.
Simmons Family Collection

Young Margaret
Circa 1900
Early program for young bicycle champion Margaret Gast.

John Nagengast

Margaret Wins CRCA Award *1901*
Award given to Margaret by the Century Road Club of America for setting the National Record, October 1901.

John Nagengast

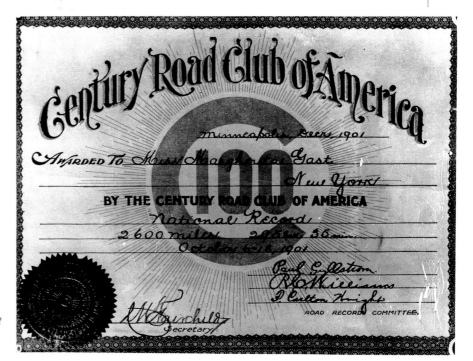

The Mile-A-Minute Girl *Circa 1910*
Promotional photo of Margaret posed on her circa 1910 Flying Merkel, billed as, *The Mile-A-Minute Girl*. Taken in Montreal, Canada. *John Nagengast*

Daredevil
Margaret in a laid-out, one-handed position on the wall. Circa 1910. *John Nagengast*

Collected Clippings
Actual page from Margaret's extensive scrapbook.
John Nagengast

The Debutante *Circa 1908*
Out-of-character portrait of a very beautiful Margaret Gast taken in New York City.
John Nagengast

Road Warrior *Circa 1910*
Margaret and her Flying Merkel, wearing one of her many gold medals. *John Nagengast*

Clara Wagner *1907*

One of the first known early American women riders in 1907, Clara Wagner was the first female issued a Federation of American Motorcyclists card. She was just fifteen. The F.A.M. was the first organized motorcycle club in America, established in Brooklyn in 1903. By 1909, membership was 3,000 strong.

The daughter of motorcycle manufacturer George Wagner from St. Paul, Minnesota, Clara was quite the accomplished rider—she

Clara on a Drop-frame *1908*
Clara Wagner on drop-frame Wagner motorcycle designed by her father.
MotorCycle Illustrated, December 15, 1908

Clara's F.A.M. Card *1908*
Clara Wagner Family Collection

participated in many activities that were entirely dominated by male riders. That is, until Clara got there.

One of George Wagner's 1909 innovations was the introduction of the first motorcycle manufactured in this country specifically designed for women motorcyclists, the Ladies' Drop-Frame Model. In addition to the metal guards over both the chain and the belt, the motorcycle featured a lowered saddle and handlebars. The special ladies model could be obtained with fabric fender skirts covering at least a full upper third of the wheels. This would supposedly keep the lady rider clean and dry. Only one of these Ladies' drop-frame models is known to exist.

On the morning of October 7, 1910, an excited eighteen-year-old Clara set off on the 365-mile F.A.M. Western District Endurance run from Chicago to Indianapolis, riding a 4-horsepower Wagner motorcycle. Clara chose not to ride the specially designed ladies model, perhaps because she needed the additional power and weight of the 4-horsepower model. Although it is said that Clara had less than fifty miles experience on this motorcycle before the run, she was an able and competent rider. She was knowledgeable enough of the mechanics of her motorcycle to make repairs if necessary, but none were needed.

According to Clara's daughter, Lucy Jacke Dettmer, "While we were growing up in California, my mom often told my brother, two sisters and I tales of this exciting escapade on her motorcycle. She said the roads were unpaved, and rough with mud, chuck holes and rocks. On several occasions, she was unable to anticipate a deep hole and she was thrown off the bike, over the handlebars and into a mud hole. Her main concern was the motorcycle and that it was still capable of continuing the race. She brushed herself off and pushed on."

Clara not only finished the run, she earned a perfect score, defeating many of her male competitors. Despite her amazing performance, she was refused a trophy because she was a woman. In protest, fifty of her fellow riders chipped in and gave Clara a gold pendant for her achievement. While the ruling body of the race had denied her credit for the race, she became the first woman in America to win a competitive motorcycle event.

In 1914, Clara married Walter Jacke, a young lawyer from Alexandria, Minnesota, who later became a county district attorney. Clara and her husband had four children and eventually moved to California. Throughout her life she loved nature and the outdoors. Clara's eldest daughter, ninety-one-year-old Dorothy Sippy recalls, "My mother's adventures did not end with motorcycling. Being an outdoor gal, she encouraged us to ride horses, play tennis and each summer she planned a month's camping in the Sierra Mountains. My dad did not like camping, so mom took us by herself. We always pitched a tent near a stream, built a campfire site and enjoyed the outdoors alone. We learned how to survive and entertain ourselves in the wilds and as I look back over my ninety years, those were perhaps my most special experiences."

Advertising Postcard Featuring Clara Wagner *1911*
Photo by A. Loeffler, Tompkinsville, New York. Card No. 30208
by Blanchard Press advertising the Eclipse Coaster Brake.

Simmons Family Collection

Clara's Scrapbook *1911*

Article from The New York Times, *January 15,*
1911: Motor Cycling Fad Strikes Fair Sex.

Portrait of Clara Wagner *1910*
Clara Wagner Family Collection

Right Off the Reel

Just as a start in the right direction the WAGNER Team entered in the CHICAGO-INDIANAPOLIS F. A. M. ENDURANCE RUN, composed of George Wagner and Miss Clara Wagner, mounted on WAGNER "4-'11" MODELS, finished the two days' grind of more than 365 miles over Indiana country roads through mud and sand with two PERFECT SCORES.

What better demonstration of the Reliability, Roadability and Riding Qualities of any machine could be asked or given than the performance of this 18-year-... machine which she had ridden ...

Clara's Scrapbook Page 1910
Clara Wagner Family Collection

No. 1, Vol. 18   TWICE-A-MONTH   15 CENTS
The Popular Magazine

ANNIVERSARY NUMBER
OCT. MONTH-END
OUT-SEPT. 25, 1910

DRAWN BY
LESTER RALPH

A SERIES OF GREAT DETECTIVE STORIES BY FAMOUS AUTHORS BEGINS IN THIS NUMBER ALSO SERIAL BY STEWART EDWARD WHITE OTHER CONTRIBUTORS~EMERSON HOUGH~ROY NORTON HOWARD FIELDING~H.C.ROWLAND AND MANY OTHERS

The Popular Magazine with Clara Wagner
on the Cover *September 25, 1910*

www.motorcyclememories.com

Wagner MOTOR CYCLES

The Real Satisfactory
"ALL-PURPOSE MACHINE"
For
BUSINESS OR PLEASURE
On Roads
Good, Bad or Indifferent
WAGNER MOTORCYCLE CO., ST. PAUL, MINN.

Wagner Advertisement *1910*
MotorCycle Illustrated, *January 15, 1910*

WHIPPLE'S MOTOR CYCLE PARTY
RECEPTION TENDERED TO DR. & MRS. C.B. CLARK
CHICAGO OPERA HOUSE
NOV 7 - 1907

Whipple's Motorcycle Party *1907*

On November 7, 1907 at the Chicago Opera House, Dr. and Mrs. C.B. Clark astonished the crowd with their thrilling motorcycle act, *The Hazardous Globe of Death*. Dr. and Mrs. Clark rode their single-cylinder Indian motorcycles round and round on the perilously narrow tracks within a sixteen-foot latticed globe at thirty-five miles an hour. Their death defying maneuvers caused even the most jaded theatergoers to sit up and gasp.

The leading motorcycle man of Chicago, Ira H. Whipple, took notice of the pair and hosted this reception and motorcycle party for them at the Opera House. At the end of the performance the audience was invited onstage to meet the Dr. and his wife, inspect the globe and the motorcycles.

MotorCycle Illustrated, *December 1907*

A Fair Yale Rider *1908*
An unknown stylish rider and her equally stylish Yale,
ready to take on the road.

Pacific Motorcyclist, *July 1, 1912*

Hazel Trumpour *1908*
Hazel Trumpour, of Chicago,
Illinois on her Magnet
Lightweight.

MotorCycle Illustrated,
January 11, 1908

the only woman motorcyclist, or—let us coin the phrase—motorcycliste, between New York and San Francisco. Through the kindness of F.H. Williams, a prominent citizen of Minneapolis, we learn that this statement is not correct, for Mr. Williams writes us that Mrs. Williams has been an enthusiastic motorcyclist for more than a year now.

This lady learned to ride the old high bicycle when fifteen years old, and on her 48-inch Champion she made a century in ten hours over Colorado roads, which was a splendid record for those days, or for any day. Afterwards, as bicycles were improved, Mrs. Williams used a safety bicycle, and in 1907, in order to be up with the times, she bought a Wagner motorcycle, which she still uses. She is thoroughly posted on the machine, for many a morning, in the wee small hours, while Minneapolis dames were yet abed, Mrs. Williams was wrestling with the mysteries of her Wagner. Mr. Williams himself has been a motorcyclist for four years. He also uses a Wagner and he says: I would not go back to pedaling if I were paid a fixed sum for each mile I covered."

Mrs. H. G. Smith—Not the Only Rider *1908*

There were very few women riding motorcycles in America in 1908. In the June, 1908 issue of *MotorCycle Illustrated*, this short article appeared:

"The unique distinction of being the only woman motorcyclist between New York and San Francisco is claimed for Mrs. H.G. Smith of Detroit, Michigan, wife of the president of the Detroit Motorcycle Club. Mr. Smith has been an ardent motorcyclist for some time, and last summer took Mrs. Smith with him on a fifteen-day run over hills, rocky roads and through peaceful valleys between Detroit and Bayport. When she returned from one of the finest vacation trips imaginable she was not only a thorough convert to the motorcycle, but decided that instead of merely being a passenger on the rear seat, she would handle the levers and brakes herself. Three months ago, she received her new machine, has now thoroughly mastered its mechanism, and accompanied the Detroit Motorcycle Club on its recent run to Cass Lake and return."

Not to be outdone, a Mr. F.H. Williams responded to this claim in the July 15, 1908 issue of *MotorCycle Illustrated*:

Not The Only One (Mrs. F.H. Williams)

"In the June issue of Motorcycle Illustrated a paragraph was printed referring to Mrs. H.G. Smith, wife of the President of the Detroit Motorcycle Club as being an enthusiastic motorcyclist for some time, and stating that she was probably

Then … more from *MotorCycle Illustrated*, August 1908:

An Intrepid Motorcycliste

"In the June issue, there appeared a short item in reference to Mrs. H.G. Smith, with the statement that she was probably the only woman motorcyclist between New York and San Francisco. But there are several others. Mrs. F.H. Williams of Minneapolis has ridden a Wagner for over a year now, and has become expert in its management. Then from Buffalo, NY, word has been received of two nurses—Misses Wardwell and Wenborne—from a Schenectady hospital, who passed through that city recently on a trip from their hometown en route to Kansas City. They were muddy and somewhat worn, but had made the run from Lyons to Buffalo, 113 miles, in one day.

Mrs. Smith, the Detroit rider, has accompanied the Detroit Motorcycle Club on several runs this spring. She also covered the seventy-nine miles from Detroit to Flint, in one day. Forty miles of this route is said to be over the worst roads in the state of Michigan. Mrs. Smith went through without a mishap, stayed with friends at Flint, and returned two days later over a different route. She rides an M.M., and she weighs only 130 pounds herself, she can travel just about as fast as any member of the club. From other parts of the country we have information of the constant use of motorcycles by lady riders, and it is pleasing to know that the softer sex are taking up this sport. They are sure to give it an impetus that would otherwise be lacking."

MotorCycle Illustrated, *August 1, 1908*

THE MOTOCYCLE NEWS

Vol. II.   SPRINGFIELD, MASS., APRIL, 1909   No. 11

C' DORA who Loops "The Globe of Death" on an Indian Motocycle
(See next page)

RISKING YOUR LIFE

Is Serious Business, and the Show Performers who do it cannot afford to make mistakes in selecting their apparatus.

There have been Four Performers in the World who Looped the "Globe of Death" on Motocycles

ALL USED INDIANS

And None Have Ever Been Injured

C' DORA

Whose picture appears on the front cover, is now appearing at the New York Hippodrome. She brought a foreign machine to this country with her, but got an Indian as soon as she could.

IT NEVER FAILS HER

Other performers have been using the INDIAN for over two years, both in this country and abroad, and to its reliability they owe their lives

MADE BY THE

Hendee Manufacturing Co.

Springfield, Mass.

The Unstoppable C' Dora *1909*

Perhaps one of the earliest records of a woman to ride in the Globe of Death in America was Miss C' Dora, who rode her Indian at the New York Hippodrome in 1909.

The Motocycle News, *April 1909*

A Ride in the Country *1909*

Beautiful farmyard scene of an unknown woman standing with a circa 1909 Erie motorcycle. Card was posted at Corning, New York on September 28, 1909.

www.motorcycle-memories.com.

Florine Travis *1909*
Taking a spin on the track of the Indianapolis Motor Speedway,
Florine Travis mounted on a Thor racing machine.

Motorcycle & Bicycle Illustrated, *August 1, 1909*

McPherson, Kansas Coeds *Circa 1910*
Photo of women perched on motorcycles taken on the grounds of the college at McPherson, Kansas.

Simmons Family Collection

No One Likes to be Shaken— Even by a Motorcycle. That's Why Those Who Ride

THE FLYING MERKEL

say: "there's no shaking here." The Spring Frame and Fork smooths out the roughest roads. Get our new catalog which tells all about them. If you're thinking "agency" post us a line today.

Merkel-Light Motor Co.
POTTSTOWN, PENNSYLVANIA
MEMBERS OF M.M.A.

Merkel-Light Motor Co. Ad *1910*
This early Merkel-Light Motor Company of Pottstown, Pennsylvania advertisement boasts "there's no shaking here".

Motorcycle Illustrated, *March 1, 1910*

Clara Inge *1910*

Vaudeville performer Clara Inge was one of perhaps thirty known women riders in the New York area in 1910. She purchased a new Harley-Davidson from the Weaver-Ebling Company, New York agents, and, according to her modest claims, did fifteen or twenty miles on the road whenever the weather permitted between shows.

"It's not nearly as hard as you can imagine, she says. I always thought a motorcycle needed a trained mechanic to manage it and a man's strength to control the handlebars. Besides it seemed a dirty pastime. I believed that you got covered with grease and grime trying to run one. Well, you just don't. I've been at it for two weeks and this suit doesn't look very mussy, does it?" The spotless garment bore out Miss Inge's statement.

The Mansfield News, *March 21, 1911, Mansfield, Ohio*

"I do not see why more women do not ride motorcycles, declared Miss Inge. I always enjoyed bicycling, but motorcycling is much more stimulating. It must be as enjoyable as flying, and I know it's safer. Until recently I imagined that motorcycle riding always soiled a person's costume, but I haven't found it so. I've been riding for two weeks, and haven't a spot on my dress yet. It's easy too; I didn't have the least trouble learning to operate my machine, and I'm just crazy over it."

MotorCycle Illustrated
January 1, 1911

MISS CLARA INGE

Astride an Unknown Motorcycle *Circa 1910*
Smartly dressed lady astride an unknown make of motorcycle.
www.motorcycle-memories.com

Alice Karslake *1911*

Alice Karslake, from Oakland, California was an intrepid rider who showed her ability and skill in endurance riding starting in 1910. In a 250 mile endurance run sponsored by the San Francisco Motorcycle Club, Alice earned a perfect score, deftly managing the challenging roads from the Golden Gate City to Monterey and back again. She checked in with husband Frank (himself a well-known rider) at the various stations. Riding over the rough roads of the San Juan grade on her trusty Merkel, Alice established a record that would not be soon outdone by any rider of her sex. She refused any special consideration throughout the run and willingly faced all hardships with grit and determination. In her own words, she describes how she distanced her husband in the early stages of the return trip and left a trail of defeated male contestants behind her:

"Our starting time was at 5:30 am, Mr. Karslake and myself being checked out together. There were twenty-six starters leaving in pairs five minutes apart. The weather was perfect, with exception that Jack Frost had been out and left his respects, making it rather chilly. It was still dark when we started, compelling us to ride an hour with lights, which made it somewhat difficult to make time until we reached the boulevard about seven miles out of San Francisco when we could ride at a fair rate, passing a few of our less fortunate contestants."

She must have really loved the rough ride, and appeared a bit stubborn as well …

"Mr. Karslake tried to persuade me to remain in Gilroy and return with the San Francisco Club, which was to hold a run there, but I convinced him that was out of the question and that I had entered to win if possible. We started riding as fast as the rough road would allow, so I could have more time, if necessary, on the much dreaded San Juan mountain, which I had never been over before. It was accomplished with much less difficulty than I had expected. I dismounted twice where others were stopped, as owing to the rough grade I could not get past them."

Alice encountered very little trouble and made it to the top of mountain. The roads from the foot of the mountain on to Salinas were very rough, but from Salinas to Del Monte the roads improved and she enjoyed the beautiful scenery. She continues …

"After leaving San Jose I rode as fast as to gain all the time I could before dark, as I had left my lamp at San Jose. Suddenly my machine stopped about half a mile from Lorenzo and I discovered I had no gasoline and no time to delay. I took the belt off and decided to push the machine in. Mr. Karslake arrived soon and wanted to assist me but I told him to go ahead and find the storekeeper and have the gasoline ready for me when I arrived. It had gotten dark by this time so we came in a roundabout way, feeling guilty at breaking the law, which compels one to ride with lights, but under no circumstances we could hardly be expected to do otherwise. Arriving in Oakland we were met by several of our friends who were much elated over my success. I felt less tired than I had expected owing to the easy riding of the Merkel machine."

Alice kept right on riding motorcycles and in 1913, with a passenger riding tandem, she rode her Harley-Davidson along a winding seven-mile trail without stopping to the summit of Mount Hamilton.

In 1914 she won a five-pound box of chocolates—an award for being the lady rider coming the farthest to a meet. She rode her twin Harley-Davidson from San Francisco, a distance of 130 miles.

Her husband Frank rode Duck motorcycles in 1907 to wins at Concord, California and was also known for his endurance and reliability contests riding Curtiss motorcycles in 1909.

MotorCycle Illustrated, *January 1, 1911*

"Cy" Woodman *1912*

In 1912, a daring New York City newspaper reporter named Miss "Cy" Woodman became known as the first woman to attempt to ride across the United States alone by motorcycle. Acting on a dare from fellow members of the Press Club and with only six lessons on the motorcycle before her departure, Miss Woodman's goal was to ride her Flanders 4 across the country, taking some time to enjoy the trip. The Flanders she rode was a 4-horsepower, built in Detroit, Michigan and had a top speed of forty-five mph.

As quoted by the *Des Moines Register* on October 31, 1912, "Cy" stated, "If a woman has a comb, a toothbrush and a nail file, she can travel most anywhere in comfort". Probably no woman ever traveled three thousand miles with such little luggage; all she took was a riding outfit: khaki riding breeches, shirt, coat and a change of clothes.

After several spills, one near Des Moines that banged her up very badly, "Cy" fell ill on the road near New Mexico, where she ended up in a hospital to have her appendix removed. According to the *Elyria Evening Telegram* dated October 21, 1913, "Cy" spent much of her time en route in hospitals and completed the trip to California by train, losing the bet she'd made with her fellow journalists. According to the article, "Several wagers were made that she would be unable to complete the trip on the machine and Miss Woodman will have to purchase several dinners to square her account."

Des Moines Register, *October 31, 1912*
Elyria Evening Telegram, *October 21, 1913*

Margaret Karslake *1916*

On April 16, 1916 the San Francisco Motorcycle Club held its third run of the season. Leading the way and riding a Cleveland was sixteen-year old Margaret Karslake. Following Miss Karslake came her mother Alice, riding a three-speed Harley-Davidson.

The sight of the two ladies riding on their own motorcycles caused quite a sensation, but the admiration went to little Margaret as she piloted her Cleveland at the same speed as the rest of the riders. The roads were rough, sand and gravel, and up and down hills and Margaret, having never ridden in the country before, completed the trip with no spills to a perfect score.

Margaret was dressed in a neat manner, wearing a close fitting cap, sailor blouse with green coat and regular riding breeches with leather leggings. Eight other ladies in the club run wore riding breeches and enjoyed themselves far more than the girls who wore skirts.

Regrettably there is no photograph to enhance the story.

Girls with Harley-Davidson *Circa 1911*

Two young ladies pose with a circa 1911 Harley-Davidson tandem single. Wearing the riding outfits of the era, including boot covers, canvas skirts and bonnets, the girls are ready to ride.

Simmons Family Collection

Merkel Rider
Circa 1911
Young lady posing
with a circa 1911
Flying Merkel.
www.yesterdays.nl

Katherine Kelly *Circa 1911*
The Goodrich tire company was well ahead of the rest when it came to promoting its products. They came up with the perfect publicity plan … they would send a woman rider across the country on a motorcycle— outfitted with Goodrich tires, of course. And Katherine Kelly of Chicago was that young woman.

On a mid-June morning in 1911, Katherine left Philadelphia on a Merkel twin fitted with brand-spanking-new Goodrich tires. Accompanied by A. G. Chapple, a renowned cross-country rider, Katherine covered an astonishing 1,382 miles in eight days and six hours, an average of about 170 miles per day. Her route led her through New York City, Albany, Syracuse, Rochester, Buffalo and Toledo.

Except for a few occasional falls which bent her pedals, and three days of rain, the ride was an unrivaled success—no doubt the longest, fastest motorcycle ride ever accomplished by a woman at that time in history. The biggest day's ride was from Syracuse to Buffalo, 216 miles. The fifty-two miles between Geneva and Buffalo were ridden in two hours despite continuous rain. The most difficult ride was between Elyria and Norwalk, Ohio, six long hours and fourteen long miles of wet, red mud—the unstoppable Miss Kelly simply rode through the fields.

The Clincher, *August 1911*
Akron, Ohio
Motorcycling, *June 29, 1911*

BREAKING THE RECORD
ON THE

GOODRICH WHITE TREAD
LARGE STUD TIRES

Miss Kelly   Mr. Chapple

MISS KELLY'S QUICK RIDE
(From Motorcycling, June 29, 1911)

MISS KATHERINE KELLY, of Chicago, who left Philadelphia about 10 a. m. June 19 on a Merkel twin, fitted with Goodrich Tires, reached Chicago at 4 p. m. on Tuesday of this week. She was accompanied by A. G. Chapple all the way and covered 1,382 miles in eight days and six hours, an average of about 170 miles per day. Her route was via New York, Albany, Syracuse, Rochester, Buffalo and Toledo.

Except for a few occasional falls, which bent her pedals, t h e ride was entirely satisfactory and is no doubt the longest and fastest road ride ever accomplished on a motorcycle by a woman.

The biggest day's ride was from Syracuse to Buffalo, 216 miles. Of this, the 52 miles between Geneva and Buffalo were ridden in two hours in spite of continuous rain. The hardest ride was between Elyria and Norwalk, Ohio, fourteen miles in six hours— wet, red mud necessitating riding through the fields in places. There were approximately three days of rain in all.

THE B. F. GOODRICH COMPANY
AKRON, OHIO

Miss Kelly at the Goodrich Branch, Philadelphia.

Katherine Kelly gets a grand send-off at the Goodrich branch in Philadelphia.

All photos, The Clincher

OVERLEAF: Chicago Motorcycle Club *1912*
Weekend outings became very popular, often including the whole family. Chicago Motorcycle Club family picnic, June 30, 1912.

Harley-Davidson Archives, copyright H-D

The Arrivals at Chicago.

Miss Kelly and escort A.G. Chapple at the end of the 1,382 mile ride.

Indian Ladies *1912*
Two riders team up on a 1912 Indian twin,
equipped with the popular tandem seat.
Simmons Family Collection

OPPOSITE: Lillian Slaughter Heaps and Grace Lester *1912*
Lillian Slaughter Heaps and Grace Lester aboard a circa 1912 Harley-
Davidson twin with often seen tandem seat and handlebars.
Harley-Davidson Archives, copyright H-D

Fashion Rebels with Excelsior Motorcycle *Circa 1912*
Two unidentified women riders with a circa 1912 Excelsior
motorcycle. These two are dressed a bit before their time.
Wearing men's trousers and newsboy hats, which most
women weren't wearing this early.

www.motorcycle-memories.com.

Unknown Woman with Thor *Circa 1912*
Unknown rider with what appears to be a 1912 Thor, a
four-horsepower single cylinder machine.
Bicycle World and Motor Cycle Review, *1912*

Vera Matthews *1912*

Vera Matthews, a noted horsewoman from Fond du Lac, Wisconsin, (who set the World's Record for the 20-mile Relay Race) also discovered the joy of motorcycling.

"I love horses and love to ride them, said Miss Mathews. But I love motorcycling too. I have watched men riding motorcycles and had for a long time wished I could ride one too. There seemed to be no reason why I should deny myself the pleasure they seemed to be getting. . . . And so I got a motorcycle. And I was right about it. Pleasure doesn't half begin to tell what motorcycling means. Now I can have both my horse and my motorcycle—and enjoy both of them."

Vera took long trips through the country in and around her home. She had no difficulty operating her machine, and believed it easier than riding a horse.

She also used her talent to help advertise the Feilbach motorcycle. The Feilbach, manufactured in Milwaukee, Wisconsin from 1904 to 1914, featured Vera in several of their advertisements.

Elyria Evening Telegram, *Elyria, Ohio, November 30, 1912*
Oakland Tribune, *January 19, 1913*
Motorcycling, *March 20, 1913*

vel That Competes in Luxury With Famous Railroad Transit

This is not a cheap machine, you will be proud to own it. This machine means to motorcycle travel what the famous limited trains mean to railroad travel, viz.: speed and luxury.

The Feilbach Limited

You can see in a minute that the Feilbach Limited has style and quality. We invite dealers, agents and riders to make a careful and critical examination of its unequalled **new features**, especially the spring fork—Longitudinal Seat Springs. We sell this high grade Limited at $250.00; 5 horsepower, long stroke motor with offset crank shaft.

WRITE TODAY FOR BOOKLET

EILBACH MOTOR CO., Milwaukee, Wis.

William Hoegee Ad *1912*
The William Hoegee Company of Los Angeles ran an ad for motorcycle clothing and accessories which featured a fetching woman rider.
Pacific Motorcyclist, *October 15, 1912*

Motorcycle Goods
FOR MEN AND WOMEN
Suits to order, Boots, Leggins, Gauntlets, Sweaters, Toques, Caps, Goggles, Kodaks.

The Wm. HOEGEE CO. Inc.
Greatest Sporting Goods House on the Pacific Coast
Main 8447 138-42 So. Main
Home 10087
LOS ANGELES

1913 to 1919

A Few Fair Motorcycle Fans

MISS. LILLIAN SLAUGHTER, MILWAUKEE

MISS. LILLIAN HAUERWAS, MILWAUKEE

MISS. PEARL. E. WILLS, CANAL DOVER, O.

MRS. W. R. DREHER, TOLEDO.

A. SEATTLE ENTHUSIAST

MRS. E. F. WINFIELD, GRAND JUNCTION, COLO.

A Few Fair Motorcycle Fans *1913* Beautiful full-page pictorial of women and their rides from across the country. *Motorcycling, March 20, 1913*

OPPOSITE: Maids and Machines *1917* Los Angeles Motorcycle Club's Ninth Annual Run to Seal Beach. *Pacific Motorcyclist and Western Wheelman, September 6, 1917*

Constance Henry *1913*

Charmer Constance Henry from Reno, Nevada rode her own Indian 4, as illustrated in this photo provided by Indian agents of the Mack Auto Company. The roads of Reno were generally good, with hard surfaces. There are numerous hills, but many level places; not a mountainous country.

Pacific Motorcyclist,
December 4, 1913

Dora Rodriguez *1913*

At nineteen, Dora Rodriguez came to America from Holland to study the educational system in the United States. She spent time doing the same in other, smaller countries, but she'd always managed to get around by foot or public transportation. America was so immense, she decided to use a motorcycle as a convenient and economical means of transportation. She became an expert at handling the machine and liked her 1913 Henderson so much that she planned on bringing it back to Holland with her when she returned.

The Des Moines News, *June 15, 1913*
National Motorcycle Museum,
Anamosa, Iowa

Lady of the Road on Emblem Motorcycle

Circa 1913

Wearing goggles and sitting on a circa 1913
Emblem motorcycle, this daring lady is road-ready.

www.motorcycle-memories.com

Minnie E. Waddell *1913*

Minnie Waddell grew up an outdoor girl, riding horses in Redlands,
California. It was an easy transition from riding horses to motorcycles
when cycling became popular. She often rode seventy-five to 100
miles in an afternoon, even climbing Mount Rubidoux in Riverside,
California. Says the independent Minnie, "Though tandem riding
is fine, it is nothing to compare with the pleasure of having a
motorcycle of one's very own, and being able to take a spin through
the open country at any and all times."

Minnie said it was a mistaken idea that motorcycles were too
heavy for a woman. Not only could she *manage* her mount with ease,
but she understood the mechanics of the machine and often made
her own minor repairs. She was also a member of the F.A.M.

Her ideal riding outfit consisted of a navy blue khaki short
divided skirt, with regulation Norfolk coat, warm bloomers and high-
laced boots.

The Des Moines News, *June 15, 1913,*
MotorCycling and Bicycling, *December 20, 1915*

Mrs. Herman Altop *1913*

"In fall of 1913, the Toledo Motorcycle Club held an endurance run of over 367 miles over rough and muddy roads through Lima, Dayton, Springfield, Fostoria and back to Toledo, Ohio. F.A.M. rules did not permit women contestants, so Mrs. Herman Altop simply rode along and made an unofficial perfect score, earning an unofficial gold medal. The ride tested the best men riders—grit and enthusiasm served Mrs. Altop well. She rode brilliantly on several tours; but she gave due credit to her faithful machine. Mrs. Altop said that from beginning to end on this tour, her Yale twin motorcycle worked like an "eight-day clock and did not miss an explosion."

Pacific Motorcyclist, *January 1, 1914*

Savannah, Georgia Motorcycle Club *1913*

Pictured are half a dozen members of the Savannah, Georgia Motorcycle Club. In 1913, there were perhaps more women members of the Savannah Motorcycle Club than any other club in the country. There were about twenty young women riders in Savannah—southern bells who were enthusiastic riders.

The Bicycle World and Motorcycle Review, *November 11, 1913*

Pacific Motorcyclist

LOS ANGELES, CAL.   AUGUST 14, 1913

Taken After Dinner

Taken After Dinner *1913*
Out for an after dinner spin on a mule and a motorcycle.
Pacific Motorcyclist
August 14, 1913

Ruth Hopper *1913*
Idaho's Ruth Hopper Beal ready to ride an Indian motorcycle.
Beal Family Collection

Yale Advertisement *Circa 1913-14*
Rare Yale advertising postcard, featuring a charming rider sporting a Yale pennant on her riding outfit. Pennants were extremely popular, featuring either the name of the favorite motorcycle, town or destination.   *www.motorcycling-memories.com*

Bessie Brucess *1914*
Portland Oregon's Miss Bessie Brucess on her Excelsior motorcycle.
Pacific Motorcyclist, *July 2, 1914*

Diamond Tire Ad
1914
Great black and white advertisement with woman riding safely in the rain on her Diamond Safety Tread tires.

Pacific Motorcyclist,
March 26, 1914

Diamond
Safety Tread
(Squeegee)
Motorcycle Tires

When you turn your machine loose for a run you like to feel somewhat sure that there will be no spills to spoil the trip. If your motorcycle is equipped with the Diamond Safety (Squeegee) Tread Tires, a quick turn, a corner rounded at a high speed, or a car track crossed at the wrong angle are robbed of their possibilities of danger by the tough rubber fingers that hang onto the roadway and *keep you right side up.*

You're certainly taking some chances when you attempt to "beat it" with other tires on muddy or wet streets, but Diamond Safety (Squeegee) Treads are the ones that will give you that "life insurance" feeling of security.

**Try
'em
out**

When "She" Rides

there is but one tire that will give her the proper degree of *safety*—that is the

Diamond
Safety (Squeegee) Tread

So, if you have a thing to do with it, see that "she" rides on *the tread with the gripping squeegees* —the tread that digs right down through mud and ooze to hard rock-bottom and *grips*—the tread that stops that skid before it even starts

The motorcyclist who uses his mount with any degree of regularity should not think of riding on anything but Diamonds. No other tire made will give you equal *safety*—no other will give you such *mileage*. We get reports of eight, nine and ten thousand miles in hard usage right along.

This is testimony that counts—you can't get away from it; *mileage and safety*—that is what you want—so if not already riding on Diamonds, equip your mount with them **at once** and see what it really means to ride "tire-care-free."

Diamond   **Motorcycle Tires**

AKRON-OHIO

Diamond Motorcycle Tire Ad *1914*

When She Rides. Advertisement for Diamond Tires aimed directly at the female rider.

Pacific Motorcyclist, *July 19, 1914*

Empire Rubber & Tire Company Ad *1914*
Empire Rubber & Tire Company advertisement featuring Mrs. J. Felix Carson, from Grand Junction, Colorado.

Pacific Motorcyclist, *July 30, 1914*

MRS. CARSON, GRAND JUNCTION, COLORADO

No Tire Trouble Whatever

Grand Junction, Colo.,
12-12-13

Empire Tire Company,
    Chicago, Ill.

Dear Sirs:—

My husband and I have taken a great many long trips over our rough mountainous roads on our Harley-Davidson, which is equipped with Empire Tires, and so far have had no tire trouble whatever, and have run the machine about four thousand seven hundred (4700) miles during the ten months we have had it.

We have nothing but praise for the Empire.

Very truly yours,

Mrs. J. Felix Carson.

EMPIRE RUBBER & TIRE CO.
Factories:
TRENTON,   NEW JERSEY

EMPIRE TUBES ARE RED

Lady with Excelsior Sidecar Rig *Circa 1914*
An unidentified woman riding a circa 1914 Excelsior with sidecar. She wears the typical riding outfit for 1914, a canvas culotte skirt with leather gauntlet style gloves and riding bonnet. *www.motorcycle-memories.com*

Maude Kern *1914*

In 1914, the audacious Maude Kern not only rode an Excelsior motorcycle from Buffalo to Detroit, she added various side trips to her journey, including one to Chicago. On the last day, she rode nearly 300 miles and reached Chicago with no problems.

Excelsior Advertising man Frederick Hart boasted, "Maude attributes her good results to the complete grip control of the Excelsior, which enables her to meet every road condition without removing her hands from the handle bar grips".

Pacific Motorcyclist, *July 19, 1914*

Lady on Indian Postcard *1914*

This card was posted on April 21, 1914 to Roseburg, Oregon. It is uncertain what the numbers indicate on the gas tank next to the Indian logo. It may be an advertising postcard from the Indian factory.

www.motorcycle-memories.com

Anna T. Hack and Claire Wells *1915*
Two friends out for a ride—a long one. Anna T. Hack and Claire Wells
of Rochester, New York, en route to Westfield, Massachusetts to visit
the Pope motorcycle factory.

Motorcycling, *May 1915*

Mrs. Bixby and Mrs. Hodges *1914*
Mrs. Bixby (front) and Mrs. Hodges were two prominent members
of the San Francisco Motorcycle Club—they organized all the club's
social functions. Their motorcycle bears a pennant boosting the new
Solano Motorcycle Club from Vallejo, the beautiful town on the other
end of the Bay.

Pacific Motorcyclist, *July 19, 1914*

Chicago Eye Shield Company Ad *1915*
An advertisement for some interesting eye protection for the lady rider.

MotorCycling and Bicycling, *December 20, 1915*

OPPOSITE: Bosch Advertisement *1915*
A stylish advertisement for Bosch Magneto Company of New York,
New York.

MotorCycling and Bicycling, *December 15, 1915*

Posed on a Bosch-
Equipt Thor Motorcycle

BOSCH

MAGNETOS COST MORE, BUT BOSCH-EQUIPT MOTORCYCLES DON'T

BOSCH Magnetos are made as good as specially schooled workmen, with special designs and the best of raw materials, can produce. Because of this excellence Bosch Magnetos have become known as the most desirable of all ignition methods. The highest priced motor cars and motorcycles in the world use only Bosch.

Because of the care, because of the selection of the best materials, the Bosch Magneto costs a trifle more than other ignition systems, but, considering its ability to serve long and well and to give efficient and reliable service, irrespective of the knowledge or attention of the user, Bosch is the cheapest ignition system known.

BE SATISFIED   The motorcycle you buy **or** sell can be Bosch-Equipt—insist   SPECIFY BOSCH

BOSCH MAGNETO COMPANY

208 West 46th Street, New York

If you are interested in the popularity of Bosch, write for a copy of "How Bosch Stands in Your Field."

Della Crewe *1915*

An adventurous Della Crewe set out from her home in Waco, Texas on June 24, 1915 to tour America. It was rare for women to ride during those days, let alone that far and on such rugged, unpaved roads. Accompanied only by her scruffy dog Trouble and 125 pounds of baggage and supplies in her sidecar, Della piloted her 1914 Harley-Davidson V-twin through a variety of road conditions and weather. Not only did she battle the usual sand, mud and terribly rutted roads of that time, she dealt with heavy rains, cold and even a severe snowstorm.

Her amazing 5,378 mile journey took her from Waco to New York City to Milwaukee, with several side trips in between. Della and Trouble took a short break before heading for Florida. Another long trek through the South would soon follow, including South American and Cuba.

Later, while riding in Panama, Della got pinched for riding without a motorcycle license. She was spared being put in the *cooler* but was ordered to appear before the mayor the next day. He was so impressed with her adventurous spirit he gave her a free pass to ride without a license.

Harley-Davidson Archives, copyright H-D

Excelsior Mom and Her Brood *Circa 1915*
Adorable children posing with Mama and her circa 1915 Excelsior
motorcycle equipped with wheel covers over the spokes. Could that
be grandma standing next to the motorcycle?

www.motorcycle-memories.com

Effie and Avis Hotchkiss *1915*

A pretty, athletic twenty-year-old, New Yorker Effie Hotchkiss often dreamt about seeing California as a little girl growing up in Brooklyn. Never one for dolls and needlework, Effie had been introduced to motorcycling at age sixteen by her brother Everett, who taught her how to ride and make repairs. She caught on quickly. After only two days of instruction, she became a skilled rider, and soon bought her first motorcycle, a Marsh & Metz. Effie excelled at the sport. In 1915, she acquired her own three-speed Harley-Davidson twin with a sidecar.

In an effort to accomplish what had never been done by any man or woman, Effie decided to ride her motorcycle across the country to California. Not only did she hope to establish a record, but also that her trip would encourage other young ladies to see that motorcycling was a healthy sport for women too.

Her mother Avis, an enthusiastic sidecar passenger, decided to accompany her daughter on the long journey in the interest of safety. Their destination would be to attend the Panama-Pacific Exposition World's Fair in San Francisco, taking their time and seeing the country. Their journey would start on May 2, 1915 from their home in Brooklyn and take them through Albany, Syracuse, Cleveland and Chicago to start. They continued through the Mississippi Valley and then toward the plains and the western states that Effie had longed to see so badly.

When asked if she had any fears about taking the long trip with her daughter, Mrs. Hotchkiss replied, "Fear doesn't bother me. I can safely trust my daughter, and I am looking forward to an enjoyable trip. We plan to camp out as much as possible and only stop at hotels when we are compelled to. I do not fear breakdowns for Effie, being a most careful driver, is a good mechanic and does her own repairing with her own tools".

Along with the necessary tools, some of the items they took with them were two rubber ponchos used as rain gear, a sleeping blanket, an automatic revolver, an ax to make a campfire, a medicine kit, and a few pots and pans for cooking.

On the two month 9,000 mile excursion, the two brave women faced bad roads, cold, extreme heat, torrential rains, floods, just about everything Mother Nature could do. While in New Mexico after running out of spare inner tubes, they cut one of their rubber ponchos to fit into the tire—a makeshift repair allowing them to ride to Santa Fe, where they replenished their tube supply. There were other repairs too, Effie had to replace a sidecar wheel using a wheel from a farm threshing machine; another time she took the fenders off the sidecar because mud locked up the wheel.

Effie and Avis made history by becoming the first women to cross the United States by motorcycle. And, in San Francisco, Effie may have set another record for the most unusual way to find love. She met her future husband when she ran into him as he tried to cross the street!

1915
Effie Hotchkiss on her Harley-Davidson.
Motorcycling, May 1915

1915
Effie and her mother Avis, in front of the Firestone Tire dealership in Ossining, New York on October 11, 1915.
Hotchkiss Estate

COMPLETE NEW YORK TO 'FRISCO SIDECAR TRIP

Miss Effie Hotchkiss and Her Mother, of Brooklyn, N. Y., Recently Snapped on the Beach of Golden Gate Park, San Francisco, Cal.

1915
Effie and Avis at Golden Gate Park, San Fransisco. In Effie's hand is a jar of water from the Atlantic Ocean, carried safely across the country to pour into the Pacific.
MotorCycle Illustrated, *November 4, 1915*

1915
The Hotchkiss motorcycle buried in deep mud.
Hotchkiss Estate

Henderson Rider from Altoona, Pennsylvania *1915*
An unknown lady out for a ride on a beautiful fall day.
MotorCycle Illustrated, *December 16, 1915*

Indian Advertisement *1915*
A wonderful color advertisement for the 1915 Indian "Motocycles" from the Hendee Manufacturing Company of Springfield, Massachusetts.

Simmons Family Collection

Mary White *1915*
Mary White of Los Angeles, California on her Indian motorcycle.

Motorcycle Illustrated, *September 16, 1915*

Milady's Wheel 1915
Unidentified woman riding
a Smith Motor Wheel.
MotorCycling and Bicycling,
August 23, 1915

The Authority of the American Cycle Trades

MotorCycling
AND
BICYCLING

Every Week   **CHICAGO U. S. A.**   **August 23, 1915**

Armstrong Breaks World's Dirt Track Records at Tacoma

Thor Presents New Three Speed Models

Excelsior Announces A New Speed Model

Motorcycle Polo in South Dakota

Cycle Trade Conditions in Southern California

Milady's Wheel

Mrs. Barley and Brood *1915*

Mrs. A.L. Barley, of Dallas Texas takes the whole family for an outing on her Indian sidecar outfit.

MotorCycling and Bicycling, *December 20, 1915*

Mrs. James Haughey *1915*

Mrs. James Haughey, wife of the Indian agent in Surrey, California, a top-notch rider, tackled all kinds of roads on her Indian motorcycle.

MotorCycle Illustrated, *November 4, 1915*

New York Sporting Goods Catalog *1915*
"Motocycle" Clothing for the woman rider. The $2.00 Ladies Tourist Cap was probably not a big seller.

New York Sporting Goods Company Catalog

Motocycle Clothing

LADIES' MOTOCYCLE OUTFIT

Outfits for women motorcycle riders consist of Norfolk jacket, skirt, bloomers and leggins. We can supply these garments in two different grades of material: "Dux-bak," a soft, pliable, olive-green cotton fabric waterproofed by the Priestly Cravenette process; and "Kamp-it," which is a cotton fabric, light weight, not waterproof but sufficiently light and comfortable to wear in the hottest weather. Each garment is carefully tailored, finely finished, and is very neat in appearance and will give excellent service.

"DUXBAK"

No. **L18.** Norfolk Jacket. A neat, comfortable, stylish garment. It is very well fitted and has an adjustable belt at waist.........................Each **$5.00**

No. **L21.** Divided Skirt. So made that it may be used either as a riding or walking skirt, as desired. The two large divisions or legs of skirt are united in front by a separate gore or panel secured by ivory buttons. This can be unbuttoned at left side, folded and buttoned on right side, making a divided skirt...Each **5.00**

No. **L22.** Bloomers. Cut very full and made with faced openings and so designed that the back may be opened without removing the garment..........Each **3.00**

No. **L24.** Leggins. Shaped to fit the leg and made of double thickness of cloth to afford sure protection. Button Style.........................Pair **1.50**

"KAMP-IT"

Made the same way as the above only of a different material as described above.

No. **WN.** Norfolk jacket. Kamp-it material.........................Each **$3.00**
No. **WD.** Divided skirt. Kamp-it material.........................Each **4.00**
No. **WB.** Bloomers. Kamp-it material.........................Each **2.00**
No. **WL.** Button Style Leggins. Kamp-it material.................Per Pair **1.00**

LADIES' OVER BLOUSE

This blouse fulfills the demand for a light garment to slip over regular waist when riding. It is made of olive drab khaki with one breast pocket and a large flat collar. It is laced in front about five inches and also eyeletted on each side of bottom to give a more comfortable fit. These are suitable for many purposes. When ordering give breast measurement.

No. **2C.** Ladies' blouse......Each **$2.50**

LADIES' TOURIST CAP

The illustration of this cap does not convey the beautiful lines it possesses. It is the most desirable tourist head covering for women. It is made of Roseberry material in olive drab color and lined with silk. The edge of the cap has an elastic which shirs it making it fit close to head and prevents any dust from getting in the hair. It can be easily rolled up and carried in the pocket or bag. The goggles are clear and well fitting. Opposite illustration shows cap with goggle peak up.

No. **3.** Ladies' tourist cap....Each **$2.00**

OPPOSITE: Pope Catalog *1915*
Stunning, colorful artwork adorns the cover of this 1915 catalog advertising the new Pope motorcycles for 1915. This extremely rare Pope literature features beautiful original artwork by celebrated artist Arthur T. Merrick. A couple pauses by an inviting stream with their Pope motorcycles.

Simmons Family Collection

Prest-O-Lite Ad *1915*

Advertisement for Prest-O-Lite featuring a woman rider.

MotorCycle Illustrated, *October 1915*

Ruth Wheatley *Circa 1915*

Ruth Wheatley on a beautiful Indian twin.

www.motorcycle-memories.com

OPPOSITE:

Prest-O-Lite Ad *1915*

Battery powered lights were just arriving for motorcycles in 1915. This advertisement features the standard carbide headlight. Our lady motorcyclist is ready to ride, easily adjusting her headlight.

MotorCycle Illustrated, *December 30, 1915*

PREST-O-LITE
For Motorcycles

The Light That Stands the Jolts

A STRONG, steady light is especially important when the road is full of ruts, bumps and gravel, with unexpected turns.

The most severe jolts and bumps do not affect your Prest-O-Lite—it throws a brilliant, unflickering light far ahead, illuminating every obstacle. It gives you confidence and enables you to "throw her open" on any road because of its steady brilliance.

Prest-O-Lite is as Sturdy as Your Motorcycle

Still Prest-O-Lite costs less to buy and less to use than any other brilliant light. It is the choice of experienced riders, everywhere. You yourself can give it any attention it may need.

We have a valuable proposition for dealers—write today

The Prest-O-Lite Co., Inc.

246 Speedway, Indianapolis, Ind.
Canadian Office and Factory, Merritton, Ont.

Prest-O-Lite Exchange
Agencies Everywhere

Prest-O-Lite Advertising is helping the Live Dealers

Motorcycle riders and buyers everywhere are being told the Prest-O-Lite Story in the big magazines, such as the Saturday Evening Post, Collier's, Leslie's, Popular Mechanics, etc. You can make this co-operation profitable to yourself by telling the Prest-O-Lite Story in your own salesroom.

The Hildabrands *1915*

Fay Hildabrand and her mother, Mrs. J. S. Hildabrand left their home in Washington, Pennsylvania on April 24, 1915 to tour the country on their Harley-Davidson with sidecar. Their destination was Denver, Colorado but they were in no particular hurry—they looked planned to fully enjoy the summer adventure.

Said Fay, "People ask us the funniest questions. They want to know who makes our riding clothes, how much it costs to travel this way and what we are doing to pay our expenses. When we tell them that we are paying our expenses out of our pockets, just the same as tourists who travel on the railroads pay their bills, they want to know what we do when we find roads that we can't negotiate. We can't answer that question because we have yet to find the road we can't get over, though we have several times been warned that 'we never would get through' certain places. We always say we'll have a glance at those 'impassable roads,' and we haven't gotten stuck yet. We have ridden in the rain several days, but it hasn't been very bad".

Motorcycling, *May 1915*

110 Dealers say
The Motor Wheel Boosts Business

When 110 busy men take time to write a manufacturer to endorse any product as a business builder, it's time for dealers generally to "sit up and take notice." 110 Cycle dealers have written to tell us how the

Smith Motor Wheel
"The Bicycle Booster"

helps to sell bicycles, accessories, cameras, fishing tackle and kindred merchandise. One Illinois sporting goods man says: "The Smith Motor Wheel in my show window brings more people into the store than any other means I have been able to discover."

A detachable Motor that will propel a bicycle at any speed up to 20 miles an hour—that can be attached in five minutes and that will run 100 to 125 miles on a gallon of gasoline — has sales possibilities that any live merchandiser can see in a minute.

We invite applications from responsible, well established dealers in open territory who will mention make of Motorcycles and Bicycles now handled, volume of business done, etc. Descriptive literature on request.

List price $60.00

Fully Protected by U. S. and Foreign Patents

A. O. Smith Co. MOTOR WHEEL DIVISION "80", **Milwaukee, Wis.**

Largest Manufacturers of Automobile Parts in the World

Warm Weather Hits Chicago—
5145 Motor Wheels Already Contracted for in Illinois

Illinois dealers have already contracted for 5,145 Smith Motor Wheels and from every part of the country are coming letters justifying recent predictions of big cycle men—that with the advent of warm weather "motor-wheeling" with the

Smith Motor Wheel
"The Bicycle Booster"

would become a craze. The Motor Wheel means so much to "outdoor" people that the demand is practically unlimited. Every member of the family is a prospect.

Attaches to any bicycle in five minutes—speeds up to 20 miles an hour—100 to 125 miles on one gallon of gasoline—travels boulevards and rough roads and climbs hills with ease.

The Smith Motor Wheel is a good, steady, profit-producer, the demand for which will increase with the passing of time.

We invite applications from responsible, well-established dealers in open territory who will mention make of Motorcycles and Bicycles now handled, volume of business done, etc. Descriptive literature on request.

FULLY PROTECTED BY U. S. AND FOREIGN PATENTS

A. O. SMITH COMPANY, MOTOR WHEEL DIVISION "59" **Milwaukee, Wisconsin**

Smith Motor Wheel Ad *1915*
Savvy manufacturers such as those at Smith Motor Wheel realized potential market for women, even back when women were still thought of as the weaker sex.
Motorcycling, *May 1915*

Smith Motor Wheel Ad *1915*
Motorcycling, *April 26, 1915*

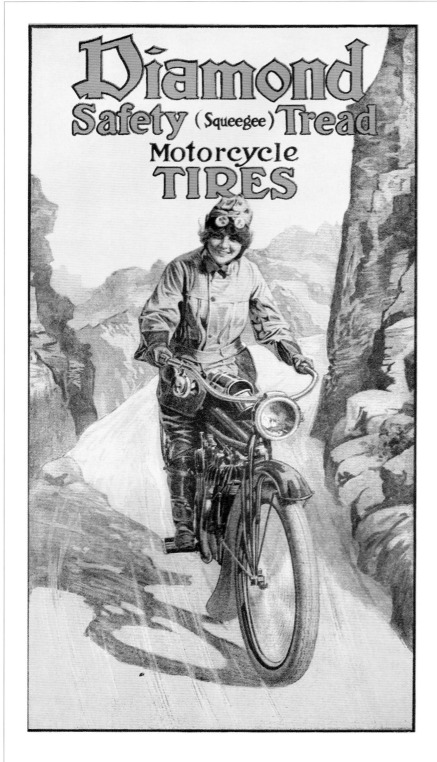

OPPOSITE LEFT: Circa Pre-1915 Advertisement for Diamond Safety Tread Tires

Colorful ad depicting woman rider descending a treacherous hill, but happy, because she is riding securely on Diamond Safety (Squeege) Tread Motorcycle Tires.

Paul Joyce Collection

OPPOSITE RIGHT: Chain Tread Motorcycle Tire Postcard

1916

A very colorful advertising postcard for Chain Tread Motorcycle Tires.

Simmons Family Collection

Excelsior Lightweight Advertisement

1916

"A practical machine for sensible riders", Excelsior Motor Manufacturing and Supply Company advertisement geared toward the lady rider who might have been interested in a lightweight model.

MotorCycling and Bicycling, April 24, 1916

COMPLETE and PERFECT HANDLE BAR CONTROL

Developed to the highest degree in the

Excelsior Lightweight

Adds the utmost degree of Comfort and Safety to the pleasure of motorcycling

Speed Control, Gear Shift and Compression Release all by levers on the handlebars so located that they may be manipulated without removing the hands from the grips or in any way interfering with the steering or any other detail of operation. All the pleasure and convenience of motorcycling without the care, attention and danger of the big and comparatively complicated models and at but a small fraction of the cost.

A Practical Machine for Sensible Riders.   See the dealer or write for catalog.

Note: If you want excessive power and terrific speed, our new Model 17-3 is a year ahead of everything

Excelsior Motor Manufacturing & Supply Co.
3700 Cortland Street, Chicago

Fair Excelsior Enthusiasts from Sidney, Nebraska *1916*
Two female Excelsior fans display their pennant.
MotorCycling and Bicycling,
May 1, 1916

Frances L. Loeb *Circa 1916*
A smiling Frances L. Loeb on her Indian Power Plus. From 1909 to 1922 Frances entered countless Endurance Runs. She was the only woman entrant in the 1922 twenty-four hour run where she had a perfect score. She also came in first in the Six Day Trials Sidecar Class.

Esta Manthos Indian Motorcycle Collection, Museum of Springfield History, Springfield, Massachusetts

Indian on an Indian *Circa 1916*
A future Indian rider on a circa 1916 Indian twin.
Only Classics

Ruth McCord *1916*

On May 6, 1916, actress Ruth McCord, the Ince-Triangle Girl, took off from Los Angeles on a 1917 Indian Power Plus motorcycle. Her goal was to complete a 25,000 mile motorcycle trip to the four corners of the United States. She set off to visit over 150 cities and over 200 Triangle Motion Picture Theaters. Ruth is said to have been the first woman to attempt to make a complete circuit of the United States on a solo motorcycle. It was a fantastic publicity stunt for the movie studio and the Indian Motorcycle Company.

1916
Ruth poses with her 1917 Indian Power Plus.

Simmons Family Collection

1916
Close-up portrait of actress Ruth McCord in her riding headgear and goggles.

Simmons Family Collection

MISS McCORD PLANTS FIRST MONUMENT

Ince-Triangle Girl on 25,000-Mile Ride to Four Quarters of United States on Indian Erects Emblem at San Diego

1916

Scene as Ruth started her trip from Los Angeles.

MotorCycle and Bicycle Illustrated, *May 31, 1917*

1917

Indian advertisement promoting Ruth McCords' cross-country ride.

MotorCycle and Bicycle Illustrated, *June 7, 1917*

MotorCycling
Cover *1916*
Colorful cover of
the whole family
out riding on a
Spring day.
MotorCycling and
Bicycling,
March 13, 1916

Two Ladies on Harley-Davidson with Sidecar *Circa 1916*
The only identification on this card is the name "Mr. Jonas Fox",
penciled into the address side of the back. The two ladies are sitting
on an early Harley-Davidson sidecar.

www.motorcycling-memories.com

1916 Prest-O-Lite Advertisement
An advertisement for Prest-O-Lite acetylene motorcycle lights. Women
riders were a huge part of their advertising in the mid teens.

MotorCycling and Bicycling, *April 24, 1916*

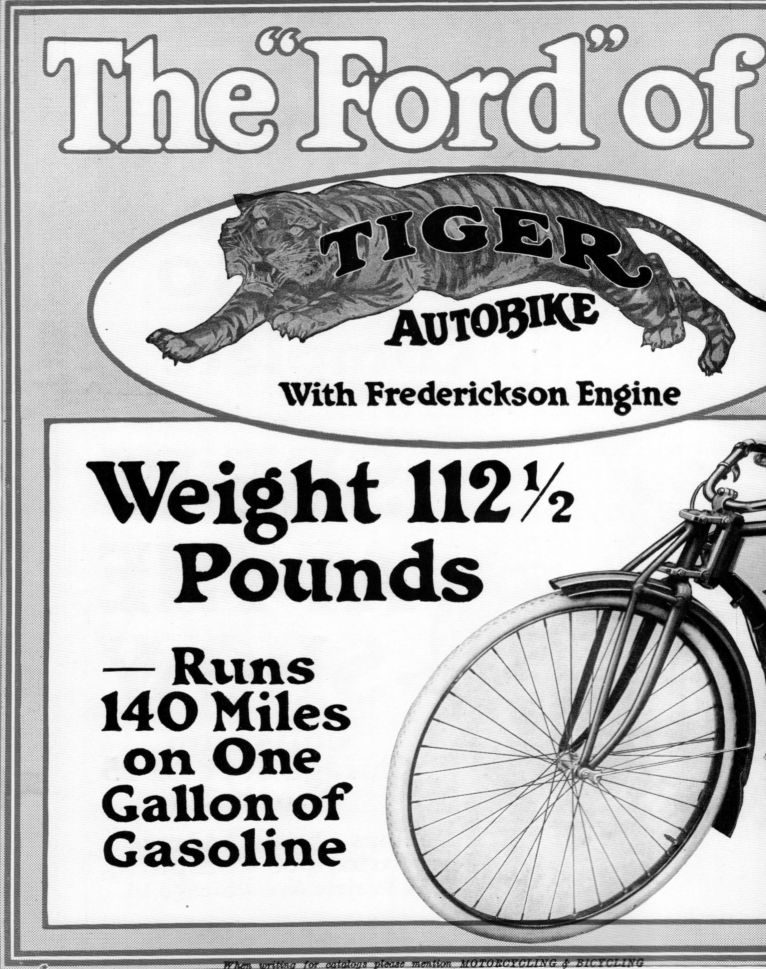

MOTORCYCLING AND BICYCLING

September 20, 1915

The "Ford" of

TIGER AUTOBIKE

With Frederickson Engine

Weight 112½ Pounds

— Runs 140 Miles on One Gallon of Gasoline

When writing for catalog please mention MOTORCYCLING & BICYCLING

Motorcycles

Price $112 50 Complete

SEE IT AT THE SHOW

Coliseum
Chicago Sept. 20-25
Booth 53

Dealers Should Address
The Autobike Company,
2231 Prairie Ave. Chicago, Ill.

Your letter gets quick action when you say, "I saw it in MOTORCYCLING & BICYCLING."

85

Augusta and Adeline Van Buren *1916*

On a cross-country ride in 1916, one would find themselves in very different conditions compared to today. Outside main cities, neglected, dirt roads were the norm. Pit stops were far apart or non-existent, and if something broke it was up to the rider to fix it. In face of these conditions, two adventurous sisters from Brooklyn, New York traveled over 5,500 miles from New York City to San Francisco in fifty-eight days.

Augusta and Adeline Van Buren, both in their twenties, were active in the National Preparedness Movement before WWI, and became interested in becoming motorcycling dispatch riders. Proving that women could ride as well as men, the two became the first women to ride solo cross-country on motorcycles. Indian motorcycles provided two Power Plus motorcycles, in return for the publicity that the women were getting for their ride.

The ride was certainly eventful and challenging. One of their many achievements was the ride up Pike's Peak, one of the tallest mountains in the Rockies. Newly completed, the dirt road was narrow, with an alarmingly steep drop to one side. They became the first women to ride to the 14,110 feet summit. Despite spills, breakdowns, and getting lost in the Utah desert, they rode into San Francisco on September 2, 1916. While their intended destinations were originally Los Angeles and San Diego, they continued down the California coast, riding into Mexico just for fun. They received big receptions in Los Angles and San Diego, but were overlooked when they rode into San Francisco.

After their cross-country adventure, the sisters were still intent on joining the military. But even after proving their abilities, courage, and tenacity, Adeline's application was rejected by the U.S. Army. Perhaps they were just too far ahead of their time.

Riding across the country in 1916 was truly a remarkable feat for anyone, man or woman. The Van Buren sisters proved what women riders knew all along, that a woman truly could ride as well as a man. Through accounts of their journey and the publicity in newspapers along the way, many a girl was likely inspired to take up riding.

Both sisters eventually married and pursued their lives. Little is known about whether they continued to ride motorcycles, but they did continue to be pioneers. Adeline, who was an English teacher, earned her law degree from N.Y.U. Augusta became a pilot, flying with the women's flying group founded by Amelia Earhart, called The Ninety-Nines.

Augusta and Adeline Van Buren broke the stereotypes of their time proving that woman could do anything a man could do. In the words of Augusta, "Woman can if she will".

The Valiant Van Buren Sisters *1916* Taken in Southern California, Augusta (left) and Adeline. Note the mudguards on the rear of the front fenders.

1916
Augusta and
Adeline in San
Diego, California.

At the Border
1916
Although
they had
accomplished the
intended scope of
their journey, they
opted to continue
down the coast
from San Diego to
Tijuana, Mexico.
Here they are on
the border at the
Terminus Cafe.
*Bob and Rhonda
Van Buren. www.
vanburensisters.com*

San Francisco Lady Riders *1916*

A group of San Francisco riders who took part in the April 16, 1916 San Francisco Club Run.

MotorCycling and Bicycling, May 1, 1916

Excelsior Ad—*A Cold Weather Kink* *1917*

Excelsior Motor Company ad featuring a woman demonstrating how to prime the motor in cold weather.

MotorCycle Illustrated, February 8, 1917

OPPOSITE: Excelsior Ad—Comfort Plus Sidecars *1917*

This advertisement for Excelsior Comfort Plus Sidecars is another of the beautiful line drawings that Excelsior was known for. This one includes a solo rider next to the sidecar.

Motorcycle & Bicycle Illustrated, July 12, 1917

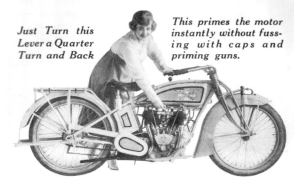

A COLD WEATHER KINK

Just Turn this Lever a Quarter Turn and Back

This primes the motor instantly without fussing with caps and priming guns.

Every motorcyclist knows what it means to start a motor in cold weather with the low grade of gasoline now obtainable.

It means prime your engine or kick your legs off.

Priming by means of a gun means delay, cold fingers and cuss words.

With the EXCELSIOR, you simply turn the priming cock located as shown in the illustration a quarter turn and back.

By this simple and instantaneous method, gasoline is delivered from the tank directly to the top of the intake valve, where it is broken into a spray and drawn into the cylinder at the first suction stroke of the motor.

In addition to this, you have the Automatic Compression Control, another exclusive EXCELSIOR feature, a combination insuring

A Start Every Time

regardless of weather or the experience of the user.

Just one of the many reasons why wise buyers buy EXCELSIORS.

Excelsior Motor Mfg. & Supply Company
3703 Cortland Street   Chicago

WHAT'S THE GOOD?

What's the good of riding far out into the country and seeking out nature's beauty spots; what's the good of purring swiftly up a hill on your Good Old **X** to arrive at the top and have burst upon your vision a brilliant panorama of sparkling lakes; what's the good of rounding an unexpected bend in the road and having laid out before your eyes a wonderful green valley of beauty; what's the good of being able to get away from the "grind" and see all of nature's wonders if there's no one along who can appreciate them with you?

The someone you take may be "the only girl" or your wife or mother, or it may be your best pal, but whoever it is they deserve to ride in comfort and ease. The

EXCELSIOR COMFORT PLUS SIDECAR

is built to fit the Good Old X—perfectly, and with it you can turn your Excelsior into a luxurious, two passenger, touring roadster.

The EXCELSIOR Sidecar combines the following details of superiority:

ALL STEEL FRAME of extra heavy seamless steel tubing and nickel steel drop forgings thruout.

EXTENSION DROP AXLE instantly adjustable to any track 44″ to 56″.

SOLIDLY CONSTRUCTED BODY, heavily upholstered with plenty of elbow and leg room and nickel plated folding foot rest.

VANADIUM STEEL SPRINGS, scroll type, front and rear and SEMI-FLEXIBLE VANADIUM STEEL SPRING CONNECTION between sidecar and motorcycle absorbs all side shocks due to inequalities in the road.

Quickly attached or detached by three bolts and is perfectly aligned at the factory. No adjustments left to the user.

PRICE $80.00 F. O. B. CHICAGO

EXCELSIOR MOTOR MFG. & SUPPLY CO.

3703 Cortland Street   Chicago

Cold Weather Cover Girl *1917*

Mrs H.G. Alexander braves winter weather on her trusty Cleveland.

MotorCycle Illustrated,
February 8, 1917

1917 Berling Magneto Advertisement

Motorcycle & Bicycle Illustrated,
November 29, 1917

MOTORCYCLE ILLUSTRATED

NEW YORK

Ten Cents a Copy

February 8, 1917

PREFERS HER LIGHTWEIGHT TO THE LUXURIES OF A LIMOUSINE

Mrs. H. G. Alexander, Wife of Treasurer Alexander of the Cleveland Motorcycle Mfg. Company, with the Machine on Which She Has Made Almost Daily Runs for Months Past.

The Key to Everywhere

When the call of Spring is in the air get out in the open.

An EXCELSIOR Motorcycle is the passport to all the beauties of nature and the key to Health and Enjoyment.

In the Series 18 line there is a machine for every purse and every purpose.

Big Powerful Twins for heavy service.
The Model L Lightweight, and the New Excelsior Side Car for touring and commercial uses.

The New EXCELSIOR catalog describes them all. Write for one or see the dealer.

EXCELSIOR MOTOR MFG. & SUPPLY CO.
3701 Cortland Street   **CHICAGO**

Excelsior Ad—Springtime *1917*
Springtime Excelsior advertisement featuring a lightweight model, rider, and a fashion-forward headband.
MotorCycling and Bicycling, *April 9, 1917*

Grace Walker *1917*
Grace Walker and her brother
Arthur pose in Washington, D.C.
for photographer Howard A.
French on their Indian Power
Plus motorcycles after their
1,000 mile ride along the coast.
Photo by Howard A. French
Motorcycle & Bicycle Illustrated,
September 13, 1917

Cleveland Rider *1917*
This Los Angeles Miss said there
was "nothing more enjoyable
than a spin" on her little
Cleveland Lightweight.
Motorcycle & Bicycle Illustrated,
March 22, 1917

Lillian Hauerwas *1917*

Lillian Hauerwas was one of the first known woman motorcyclists in Milwaukee, Wisconsin. She was one of the most prominent lady riders in the teens, working in the offices of the Harley-Davidson Motor Co. from 1916 to 1920. Lillian was also a very involved member of the Milwaukee Motorcycle Club and participated in many of their tours of southeastern Wisconsin.

She often rode her motorcycle the ninety miles to Chicago to visit family friends, despite bad roads and few places to stop for food and gas. Lillian was truly a pioneer of her time.

This essay by Lillian Hauerwas appeared in *Motorcycle Illustrated* on September 16, 1915:

"Can a girl ride a motorcycle and still retain every characteristic that is expected of our best young womanhood? I certainly believe so, and my observations cover several years. There is no danger and no coarsening influence incidental to motorcycling unless the rider deliberately injects those elements into the sport. The girl who enters a basketball game, for example, is far more likely to be hurt, and to give way to impulses not exactly ladylike than is the girl who goes motorcycling. Still many careful parents encourage their daughters to play basketball.

"Whatever prejudice exists against the use of the motorcycle by girls is due to lack of knowledge on the part of the objectors. I have found the motorcycle a safe, healthful and ever fascinating vehicle, and I feel certain that I can bring any biased parent around to my way of thinking in a ten-minute demonstration. As far as the girl rider is concerned, motorcycling is just what she makes it- and it is so easy to make it simply a pleasant, refreshing and economical pastime that I constantly wonder why more girls do not avail themselves of it".

The Des Moines News, *June 15, 1913*

Harley-Davidson Archives, copyright H-D

Clothes for the
Lassie *1917*

MotorCycle Ilustrated,
April 12, 1917

For the Girl In the Saddle

Clothes for the Motorcycle Lassie a Problem of Even Greater Importance Than with the Male Rider; It's Hard to Find Attire That Combines Modesty, Style and Durability

Motor Cycle Illustrated's "Editress" Designs the Ideal Suit for the Female Rider

By EDYTHE VAN

IT'S a trifle hard, girlie, for most folks to reconcile the accepted feminine attributes of modesty, shyness and real "lady-like" behavior, with motorcycle riding.

And, sorry as I am to admit it, I must say that but few of the feminine riders who have learned to love the two-wheeler sport—who have let motorcycles and motorcycling get under their skin and become a part of their very lives—are doing aught to make the general public take more kindly to the "girl in the saddle."

That's a matter to which I have devoted a great deal of attention this spring. And I have just about decided that while we can safely admit, in a fair proportion of cases, that "clothes do not make the man," substitute "woman" in that time-worn adage, and you are sailing dangerously close to the rocky shore of prevarication—yes, and with all sail set and Old Neptune in choppy mood.

Applied to the girl, the adage is a clean fib; that's all. You can be the nicest, prettiest, most modest girl imaginable; but just slip on a spotted khaki skirt, a somewhat soiled "middy," pull a peaked cap on backwards over your mussed hair, and go out for a ride and see if anyone not knowing you will believe it. Indeed they will not, never!

Appearance All Important

Now that's a mighty important point for the girl motorcyclist to consider. The young man can appear in soiled sports clothes and, in most cases, "get by," to resort to the vernacular. But let the girl look just the least bit slovenly and folks will think her coarse and "tough"; and no girl cares to be looked upon in that light.

The question of clothes with the male rider is all important, there's no doubt about that. It is, however, even more important with the young lady. Yet a thorough search of the market which I made this year reveals that there is nothing in the line of suitable clothes for the young lady rider that could be touched at nominal cost.

Of course there is the khaki divided skirt and a coat to match. But I have found the divided skirt not only quite inconvenient, but also far less modest for the girl who rides than the riding breeches which have come so much in vogue for the girl on horseback. Also, khaki is not the ideal fabric for motorcycle use by any means, from the standpoint of either appearance or durability.

And style! My word, but the average coat that is offered to the girl rider for motorcycle use certainly has the "Plain Jane" look that would discourage any girly with a leaning toward "niftiness" in appearance from even thinking of taking up the sport.

Some Trade Cooperation

And, just because I could find nothing that exactly fitted my needs and my taste at the same time, I decided to take my own ideas of what proper attire for the girl rider should be to some specialist in sports clothing and have a suit made up exactly to my liking. Baker, Murray & Imbrie, Inc., 15 Warren street, New York, was the firm I went to because they specialize on sports clothes and through their kindness I was put in touch with Loewenberg & Co., Newark, N. J., at whose plant my suit was manufactured.

Choice of Fabrics

I decided, first of all, that forestry cloth was the material I wanted.

I decided to have a little Norfolk jacket made with just as little shaping as the tailor could give me without making the style too severe. I decided also to have the belt raised rather higher than ordinary and to have the coat cut just as short as is consistent with modesty.

The tailor got the idea on the instant and gave the coat an added touch of style with pockets cut somewhat out of the ordinary and fitted with little buttoned flaps to cover the openings. He also fitted a collar on the "mannish" order with lapels that can be buttoned over to protect the neck and chin when the "chilling wind doth blow," to wax poetic.

Three Views of Motor Cycle Illustrated's Ideal Costume for the Young Lady Motorcyclist

Here she is, boys! She lives in Washington, D. C. If you ever get to go to Congress, you may see her flitting down Pennsylvania avenue. She is Miss Berg and she says she never even stops to powder her nose but just hops on and away she goes. However, she qualifies for the neat rider brigade

Miss Berg *1917*

Miss Berg, Secretary to P.M. Corr, the Cleveland motorcycle dealer in Washington, D.C., on her Cleveland, on which she made daily trips to and from the office.

MotorCycling and Bicycling, August 13, 1917

Mrs. Harry G. Mason *1917*

Mrs. Harry G. Mason of Newark, New Jersey with her son Harry Jr. in the sidecar. She had been riding her Excelsior with sidecar for the past three years.

Motorcycle & Bicycle Illustrated, March 15, 1917

Mrs. John Lang *1917*

Mrs. John Lang of Waterbury, Connecticut worked alongside her husband, the local Harley-Davidson agent for many years. To her, changing a tire was a simple task. Mrs. Lang was reported to be the most accomplished woman mechanic in the country at the time.

Motorcycle & Bicycle Illustrated, December 6, 1917

Mrs. M. Christiansen *1917*

"Mrs. M. Christiansen, of Bronx, New York attracted a lot of attention lately throughout the metropolitan district with her Indian-Cygnet motorcycle. In 1916 she has rode at least 7,500 miles, including the 1917 Gypsy Tour to Mount Beacon, carrying her mother and two children along.

Her motorcycle combination was fully equipped and represented a total investment of about $800. The Cygnet body was upholstered in cretonne, and boasted a flower vase, electric light and some of the other luxuries ordinarily confined to the automobile limousine."

Motorcycle & Bicycle Illustrated, *December 6, 1917*

Washington D.C. Riders *1917*
Washington D.C. Riders participating in a Gypsy Tour to Hagerstown, Maryland.

Motorcycle & Bicycle Illustrated, *July 12, 1917*

MOTORCYCLING AND BICYCLING

$1.00 A YEAR **CHICAGO** **NOVEMBER 9, 1918**

Agnes Goudy *1918*
Gracing the cover
of *MotorCycling and
Bicycling* magazine,
Agnes Goudy poses
proudly on her
Excelsior motorcycle.
MotorCycling and
Bicycling,
November 9, 1918

*Miss Agnes Goudy of Los Angeles is another member of the fair sex to adopt
the motorcycle as the ideal means of travel and recreation during the war*

Antwerp, Ohio *August, 1918*
Unknown riders on a Harley-Davidson tandem.

Simmons Family Collection

Emma Parritt *1918*
Emma Parritt of Worcester, Massachusetts, practiced speeding before her wedding day. Here, she receives a lecture on the rules of the road by an officer.

MotorCycling and Bicycling,
January 12, 1918

Esther A. Crosse *1918*
Esther A. Crosse, of Paterson, New Jersey was the first woman in New Jersey to apply for motorcycle operator's license under a new law passed in 1917. Her machine was a 1917 3-speed Indian with a Cygnet rear car outfit. She averaged about thirty-five miles, with the car loaded, on a gallon of gas. Her car was always full of members of her family, her friends and neighbors, or those she chanced to overtake on the road.

MotorCycling and Bicycling,
November 2, 1918

Maude Irons *1918*

Maude Irons was a motorcycle saleslady and rider with the Henderson
agency in Providence, Rhode Island. Ahead of her time, Maude was
the only girl in Providence who dared to wear such an outfit.

MotorCycling and Bicycling, *October 26, 1918*

Motorcycle Fashion *1918*

A good example of what kind of clothing women motorcycle riders
may have worn back in 1918.

Simmons Family Collection

MotorCycling and Bicycling
Advertisement *1918*
A little in-house advertising, with two ladies riding a Cleveland motorcycle.

MotorCycling and Bicycling,
January 12, 1918

Mrs. E.T. Latterman *1918*

Mrs. E.T. Latterman, of Park Ridge, New Jersey was an enthusiastic motorcyclist who believed in good fellowship on the road. She said, "I never pass a rider on the road if he is alone and in trouble. I always stop. My knowledge is not very great, but if I can't do any more I might be able to loan a wrench or a pair of pliers. I wear a boy's knickerbockers suit, of mixed material, with black puttees and black shoes—always polished, black gauntlet gloves, black and white small peaked man's cap altered with an elastic in the back to fit tight in a high wind, an army khaki flannel shirt, four-in-hand tie and brown goggles—and a smile. I have never had any disagreeable experience with my machine and am always treated as a lady wherever I go".

Motorcycle & Bicycle Illustrated, *January 24, 1918*

Mrs. John E. Hogg *1918*
Mr. and Mrs. John E. Hogg, of Los Angeles, Smith Wheel enthusiasts, enjoyed twenty-five miles of recreation with a quart of gas.

MotorCycling and Bicycling, *September 28, 1918*

Smiling Lady Riding Harley *Circa 1918*
Unknown woman riding her circa 1918 Harley-Davidson sidecar rig.

Simmons Family Collection

Sterling L. Britton *1918*
Sterling L. Britton of Garden City, Long Island, was assigned to the Quartermaster's Department at Camp Mills. She often used her motorcycle to assist in performing her duties.

Motorcycle & Bicycle Illustrated, *November 21, 1918*

United States Tire Company Ad *1918*
During wartime women had to work harder to make up for many of the men being away at war. In this ad for motorcycle tires, at least they got to ride too!

Motorcycle & Bicycle Illustrated, *October 3, 1918*

MotorCycling and Bicycling

$1.00 A YEAR   **CHICAGO**   NOVEMBER 16, 1918

Off for an afternoon with the local Red Cross. It is a jaunt of half a mile, but five gallons of gasoline will take her there and bring her back every day for a year

MotorCycling and Bicycling

$1.00 A YEAR — CHICAGO — DECEMBER 14, 1918

Miss Jane Erol, a Los Angeles Movie Actress, out for a spin in the country

Edna Conklin *1919*

Miss Edna Conklin of Rochester, Minnesota smiles as she takes a ride on her Harley-Davidson sidecar outfit.

Motorcycle & Bicycle Illustrated, *March 6, 1919*

OPPOSITE: Briggs & Stratton Advertisement *1919*

A vibrant advertisement for the New Briggs & Stratton Motor Wheel, formerly known as the Smith Motor Wheel.

Motorcycle & Bicycle Illustrated, *July 31, 1919*

Dorothy Vernon and Frances Delage *1919*

Dorothy Vernon, left, and Frances Delage, Los Angeles girls who toured the great state of California on their Cleveland motorcycles.

MotorCycling and Bicycling, *January 18, 1919*

Gold Star Parade *1919*
A driver proudly escorts her passenger in New York City's Gold Star Day Parade honoring veterans of the Great War.

Motorcycle & Bicycle Illustrated, *May 15, 1919*

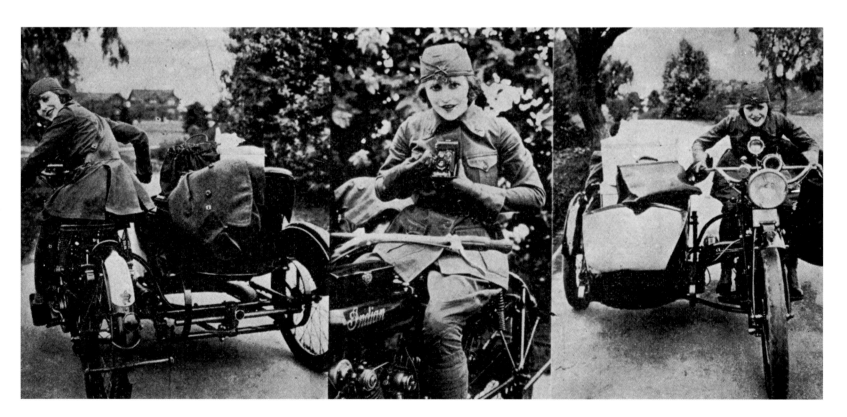

Ruth Roland *1919*
Ruth Roland, silent screen actress, who made her movie debut in 1909, was known for her love of motorcycling. Known as the Queen of the early movie serials, between 1909 and 1927 Ruth appeared in more than 200 films.

Motorcycle & Bicycle Illustrated, *December 25, 1919*

Norma Talmadge *1919*

Silent film actress Norma Talmadge was born in Niagara Falls, New York in 1897. She started making movies at fourteen years of age and became quite successful as a motorcyclist as well as a movie star.

Sid Grauman began construction on his sumptuous Chinese Theatre on Hollywood Boulevard in 1927. During construction, Norma Talmadge accidentally walked across a wet slab of cement... and inadvertently inspired the tradition for which the theater is most famous. Hundreds of celebrity handprints and footprints (and *otherprints*) now endow the concrete forecourt. Grauman's Chinese Theatre remains among the most popular tourist attractions in Southern California.

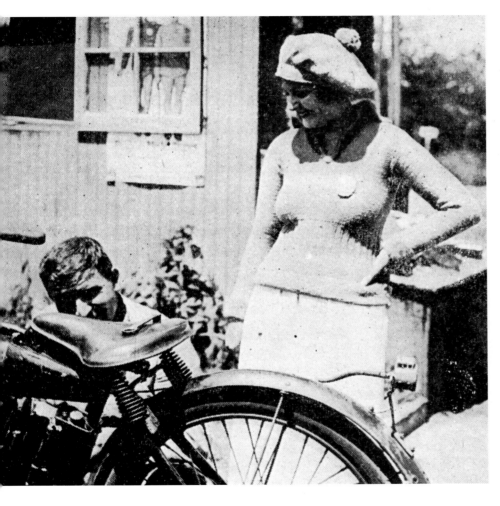

While living in Bayside Long Island, Norma was so annoyed by curiosity-seeking motorists trespassing on her property, that she complained to the Bayside authorities that a patrol was needed. Having witnessed Miss Talmadge ride her motorcycle with such speed and control, that even practiced motorcycle cops couldn't match, they immediately appointed her to the job. The shiny medal on her sweater is her license. This license enabled Miss Talmadge to stop speeding motorists and keep rabble-rousers off the beach.

Motorcycle & Bicycle Illustrated, *April 3, 1919*

Norma up close in the Chinese Theatre in Hollywood. *1919*
Moving Picture World Magazine, *April 19, 1919*
Simmons Family Collection

1920 to 1929

Ace Rider *1920*
An unidentified rider from Holyoke, Massechusetts
on a beautiful Ace motorcycle.

   Motorcycle & Bicycle Illustrated, *November 4, 1920*

Catherine Doyle *1920*
The girls of Ed Wynn's Carnival Co. purchased
several of Johnson Motor Wheels, which they
carried around during their tour of the Western
States. Pictured is actress Catherine Doyle arriving
at the theater in style.

   MotorCycling and Bicycling *October 13, 1920*

OPPOSITE: Indian Scout of 1929
"All driver motorcycle."

   Simmons Family Collection

Easter Walters: *Try this on your Harley-Davidson!*
Simmons Family Collection

Easter Walters on a circa 1921-1923 Harley-Davidson Sport Model.

In the late teens and early twenties silent film actress Easter Walters appeared in such films as *The Tiger's Trail* and *The Devils' Riddle*. She was often seen riding around Hollywood on her motorcycles. She also mastered the art of trick riding and did many of her own stunts.

www.motorcycle-memories.com

Actress Easter Walters, leaving for the studio.

www.motorcycle-memories.com

Startling New Invention For The Cycles Industry

THE above picture shows the first American built Motor Scooter—the new product which has fired the enthusiasm of jobbers, dealers and consumers the country over.

It is the Briggs-Stratton Motor Scooter, consisting of a sturdy, cut-away frame propelled by a Briggs-Stratton Motor Wheel. The wheels are 20 inches in diameter, giving a low center of gravity which makes riding easy, safe and simple. The frame, being cut out, makes the Motor Scooter very comfortable to ride. It also includes a foot-brake which facilitates stopping and handling in traffic. A large double acting spring seat and spring foot board provide ease and comfort in riding.

The power is contained in a standard Briggs-Stratton Motor Wheel which is the rear wheel. This arrangement absolutely prevents any oil or exhaust fumes from soiling the clothes. The control is on the handlebars. You simply push the motor Scooter a few feet to crank—hop on and scoot away. It gives a speed range of from 2 to 25 miles per hour with the amazing economical feature of 100 miles per gallon of gas.

Doesn't that strike you as one of the best selling propositions that has ever been offered to the Cycles Industry? It is a product that appeals to men, women and children—for pleasure, utility and commercial use. It has a tremendous market, absolutely untouched as yet. And the men who handle it are going to make the most comfortable profits they've known for a long, long time.

We would like to tell you more about its great potential possibilities—and our generous merchandising plan. Write us today for details and get the agency in your town. Don't wait. The opportunity is here—write or wire for it.

BRIGGS—STRATTON MOTOR SCOOTER
BRIGGS & STRATTON COMPANY-MOTOR WHEEL DIVISION
GENERAL OFFICES AND WORKS — MILWAUKEE WISCONSIN, U.S.A.

Briggs & Stratton Motor Scooter Ad *1920*

The motor scooter was a new creation for the cycling industry by Briggs & Stratton Motor Scooter. It was marketed for the whole family.

MotorCycling and Bicycling, *October 20, 1920*

See America on a Cleveland

The road that runs past your home leads to every place in the world. The Blue Book shows you every turn on the way to everywhere. The Cleveland 20 will take you there, carefree, comfortably, quickly, quietly and cheaper than you can get there by any other way.

All the scenery in the world is waiting for you

Plan your vacation via Cleveland Motorcycle. Equally suitable for women and men. Light, simple, manageable, trouble-free, safe, always ready. Goes three miles for a cent at the average price of gasoline. Goes wherever there's a road.

Goes where automobiles and railroads can't go. Goes as fast as you like, and you stop where you like, as long as you like. Get the atmosphere. Highroads and byways call. The Cleveland 20 enables you to accept nature's invitation.

See your dealer now for Spring Delivery

THE CLEVELAND MOTORCYCLE MFG. CO.
Cleveland U.S.A.

MOTOR CYCLE Cleveland

This advertisement appears in the
April Issue of Popular Mechanics

Cleveland Motorcycle Advertisement *1920*

Boasting seventy-five miles to a gallon of gas, the 1920 Cleveland motorcycle was a way to take a vacation and save money.

MotorCycling and Bicycling, *March 3, 1920*

Firestone Ad *1920*

A combination you can't beat, the right girl, a Cleveland and Firestones tires. This Firestone advertisement shows that you can have it all.

MotorCycle & Bicycle Illustrated, *April 1, 1920*

Frankel Leggings Ad *1920*

An advertisement for Frankel leggings, featuring female rider Laura Bromwell.

MotorCycle & Bicycle Illustrated, *November 4, 1920,*

Girl Harley Rider *1920*
Another happy motorcycle rider aboard a circa 1920 Harley-Davidson.

Simmons Family Collection

Helen Holmes *1920*
Movie star Helen Holmes, who made over ninety-two movies from 1912 to 1926, was frequently seen riding an Indian motorcycle around Philadelphia.

Motorcycle & Bicycle Illustrated, *January 22, 1920*

Miss Hazel Bilty *Circa 1920*
Miss Hazel Bilty, who was also a champion swimmer and skater, enjoyed motorcycling in Milwaukee, Wisconsin on her Harley-Davidson twin.
Harley-Davidson Archives, copyright H-D

Kathryn Adams *1920*
Actress Kathryn Adams rode her Harley-Davidson in the 1920 movie *The Best of Luck*.
Motorcycle & Bicycle Illustrated, November 18, 1920

Scene From
The
Best
of
Luck
Kathryn Adams
Features
With Her
Harley-Davidson

Indian Scout

The King of Solo Machines

Born one year ago in the Engineering Department of the vast INDIAN factory, the INDIAN SCOUT was hailed with enthusiasm, a wonderful future was prophesied and it was pronounced as representing the highest conception of mechanical perfection.

Now, one year from its debut, the INDIAN SCOUT is accepted as the king of solo machines— a wonder of engineering knowledge and mechanical skill.

It has stood the "gaff" and won the hearts of thousands of riders, not only for pleasure touring and all around utility work, but in competition as well. In endurance runs, hill climbing and economy events, the SCOUT has been a persistent winner in its class.

Today the INDIAN SCOUT holds the world's 24-hour road record—1114½ miles. The last 10½ miles were covered in 11 minutes. This is 250 miles better than the previous record.

The accomplishments of the INDIAN SCOUT are truly phenomenal. It has reached the top of

Multnomah Falls, a performance heretofore undreamed of with any form of vehicle. It has scaled Long's Peak in the Rockies to a point two miles higher than has ever been reached by any vehicle or the skilful mountain-climbing burros.

There are twice as many INDIAN SCOUT models in use in this country today as all other middleweight machines, and this has been accomplished in one year.

We are starting on our second season's production of INDIAN SCOUT models with a firm conviction that at the end of this season there will be three times the present number in use.

The INDIAN SCOUT is a bold departure from the old orthodox design of the middleweight motorcycle, but on sheer merit it has proved conclusively that it is correctly designed.

Its beauty, wonderful power and economy features, coupled with its delightful easy riding qualities, have brought it to the front a leader unrivaled.

The INDIAN SCOUT is so easily handled that it is suitable and enjoyed by the daintiest of feminine riders, while its bulldog strength and power appeal to and satisfy the hardened and experienced endurance riders.

For Proof Ask Anyone Who Has Ridden An Indian Scout

Hendee Manufacturing Company
(Largest Motorcycle Manufacturers in the World)
SPRINGFIELD, MASSACHUSETTS

Indian Scout Two-page Ad *1920*
Two page Indian Scout advertising spread featuring a handsomely dressed woman rider.
MotorCycling and Bicycling, *October 20, 1920*

OPPOSITE: Johnson Motor Wheel *1920*
Turn any woman's bicycle into a Women's Motor Bike. The Johnson Motor Wheel was the only two-cylinder motor in the world to drive a bicycle.
Motorcycle & Bicycle Illustrated, *August 5, 1920*

The Johnson Motor Wheel makes out of

a woman's bicycle the only successful Two-Cylinder Women's
Motor Bike in the world. The demand for an individual vehicle
of motor transportation for women becomes more insistent daily.

The Johnson Twin
is the only Two-
Cylinder Motor
in the world to
drive a bicycle.

On a woman's Johnson Motor Bike the flat twin-cylinder double
opposed engine, electric light generator and gasoline tank are so
placed in rear of the rider that there can be no annoyance, discom-
fort or dirt from the motor.

The illustration at top is a correct portrayal of a young lady on a
Johnson Motor Bike showing the exact position of the power plant
and the ease with which she handles the machine.

In riding the Johnson Motor Bike, ladies do not have to wear any
special motor clothing for protection from the operation of the motor.

150 miles on a gallon of gasoline. 6 to 35 miles an hour. No
pushing. Coast uphill as well as down. Simple and easy to
handle. Ask us about it.

THE JOHNSON MOTOR WHEEL COMPANY

916 East Sample Street · · · · · South Bend, Indiana

Mabel Normand *1920*

Silent film actress Mabel Normand was probably better known for her love of fast cars than motorcycles. Here she is pictured at the Sam Goldwyn Studio lot in Culver City, California around 1920 posing with an Indian Power Plus.

No one really knows if she rode a motorcycle off-screen, but in 1914's *Mabel at the Wheel*, which Mabel starred in and co-directed with Mack Sennett, the villainous Charlie Chaplin offers Mabel a ride on his motorcycle—but drops her in a puddle.

Mabel at the Wheel
Mabel Normand and Charlie Chaplin co-star in *Mabel at the Wheel*.

Simmons Family Collection

Mabel in the Mud
This scene shows Mabel falling off the back of Charlie Chaplin's motorcycle.

Simmons Family Collection

Looking for Mabel *Circa 1920*
Mabel showing some flexibility on her motorcycle.

Marilyn Slater of Looking for Mabel

Mabel and the Indian *Circa 1920*
Goldwyn star Mabel Normand on her Indian motorcycle.

MotorCycling and Bicycling, March 14, 1920

Circa 1920
Mabel reads up on how to adjust her carburetor.

Marilyn Slater of Looking for Mabel

Motorcycle & Bicycle Illustrated

Ten Cents A Copy

April 29, 1920

Spring Days are Pleasure Days

Spring Sports Number

Cover Girls
1920
Cover of a spring issue showing two women enjoying the day on their Motor Wheels.
Motorcycle & Bicycle Illustrated
April 29, 1920

Mother and Baby *1920*
A young mother and her baby out for some fresh air on her Briggs & Stratton motorized bicycle and sidecar.
MotorCycling and Bicycling, *March 14, 1920*

Mrs. Floyd Clymer and Mrs. John E. Bice *1920*
Mrs. Clymer of Denver, Colorado and Mrs. Bice, of Detroit, Michigan on Evans Power Cycles, attending the annual motorcycle show at Chicago Coliseum. Mrs. Clymer was married to Floyd Clymer, renowned rider, racer, writer and motorcycle salesman for many years.
Motorcycle & Bicycle Illustrated, *November 18, 1920*

Mrs. Oscar Lenz *1920*
The wife of famed hill-climber Oscar Lenz, Mrs. Lenz believed that men shouldn't monopolize the art of climbing. She took a sidecar outfit with her friend and passenger Mrs. F. Wertz over the top.

MotorCycling and Bicycling,
July 28, 1920

Ner-A-Car Girls *1920s*
The Ner-A-Car, designed by J. Neracher, was produced between 1921 and 1926 in England and America. Small and easy to ride, the Ner-A-Car was marketed as a second, inexpensive mode of transportation for families. Some 1925 and 1926 models came with mudguards and bucket seats. It was so easy to handle, girls could even ride it in their bathing suits! *OnlyClassics*

Mrs. Roy J. Smith *1920*

In an admirable exercise in marital togetherness, husband and wife duo Mr. and Mrs. Roy J. Smith made a 2,000 mile trip from Newark, New Jersey to Miami, Florida. Mrs. Smith earned a long-distance tour medal. She was the first woman driver to compete in a second-class tour, and won a silver medal for long-distance touring.

1920
Mr. and Mrs. Roy J. Smith on their Harley-Davidson twin.

1920
Some of the tough going for Mrs. Roy J. Smith on her recent trip from Newark, New Jersey to Miami, Florida. Many of the roads were unpaved and very muddy.
All photos MotorCycling and Bicycling, *March 3, 1920*

Doris Gray and Barney Paige *Circa 1920s*
Doris Gray and Barney Paige rode the wall in the
1920s. They married soon after this photograph
was taken and rode in the big *silodrome* with the
Keystone Exposition Shows.

OnlyClassics

Sextette of Lady Rider's at Stern's Picnic *1920*
The roar of over 330 motorcycles filled the air as they rolled past green fields toward the Stern brothers' picnic in rural Westchester, about forty miles outside of New York City. The day was filled with races and field events. Pictured in these six photographs are the solo women riders whose arrival caused quite a stir:

Bessie Hollander, New York City
All photos MotorCycling and Bicycling
May 26, 1920

Above: Florence Werner, New York City

Left: Edna Berkley, Newark, New Jersey

Above: Jennie Cummings, Hackensack, New Jersey

Left: Freda Greenwald, New York City

Laura Bromwell, also a licensed aviatrix, from New York

Lillian Farrow *1920s*

Lily Farrow, born in 1892, was the wife of one of the first and most prominent Harley-Davidson dealers in the country, Alford D. Farrow. When he was only twenty-three years old, A. D. opened his first dealership in 1912 in Nelsonville, Ohio. In 1925 he moved it to Columbus, Ohio. A. D. passed away in 1927, leaving Lily to run the shop—America's first woman motorcycle dealer. Besides running the shop, Lily also had three small children to raise, Bob, Jane and Don.

For many years, Lily was the only woman motorcycle dealer in the country. She hired a man named Harold Kinnel to help. They managed to keep the business going during the Second World War by selling used bikes and services instead of new—Harley-Davidson was producing motorcycles solely for the military during the war years.

Several years later Lily and Harold were married. Eventually they retired, and the Farrow dealership was turned over to Lily's son Don and his wife Dorothy. From there, the shop was handed down to Don's son Robert and in 1983 it was sold to Al and Pat Doerman. In 2003, the dealership was sold to its current owners Bob and Valerie Althoff. Still called A. D. Farrow Co. Harley-Davidson, it's America's oldest continuously operated Harley-Davidson dealership. The shop will celebrate its 100th anniversary in 2012.

Buckeye Motorcycle Club *1940*
Club Member Lily Farrow, second from right.
A. D. Farrow Co.

Circa 1914
Portrait of a young Lily Farrow.
A. D. Farrow Co.

Circa 1915
A. D. and Lily Farrow on a Harley-powered bobsled. "Motor Bobbing" was a popular
winter activity for many Harley enthusiasts, in the early years.

A. D. Farrow Co.

Jane Farrow Langley

To Jane Farrow, being around motorcycles was as natural as breathing—she'd been living with Harley-Davidsons ever since she could remember. Her father A. D. died when she was just three years old; she and her two brothers grew up in the motorcycle dealership her widowed mother took over. She says she was "born with the sound of motorcycles" in her ears, and as she got a little older, she worked in the shop right alongside the boys. Older brother Bob taught her to ride. She got her first motorcycle just after she graduated high school—a Harley with chrome tanks, fenders and red leather saddlebags. She loved the bike, and the many adventures she had on it.

Jane and her Aunt Nellie Jo Gill rode in tandem to visit the 1939 New York City World's Fair. The people they encountered were amazed that two women would make such a trip.

Eventually Jane joined the Army Air Corps, where she met Bill Langley, a decorated fighter pilot. She married Bill in 1945; their union lasted sixty-three years. After getting out of the service, they opened their own Harley-Davidson dealership. Around this time Jane met Dot and Earl Robinson, also Harley dealers. Dot was president of the Motor Maids. Jane joined the Motor Maids as well, and a close friendship was born.

Jane continued to ride for many years and as of this writing in 2009, is still a member of the Motor Maids, the club she joined in 1943. She still enjoys going to the conventions to see her old friends.

1942
Jane Farrow Langley in her Buckeye Motorcycle Club uniform.

Jane Farrow Langley

1939
Jane Farrow riding passenger with her aunt, Nellie Jo Gill on the day they left Ohio for the World's Fair in New York.

Jane Farrow Langley

1939
Jane Farrow and Nellie Jo Gill featured on cover of *American Motorcyclist* magazine.

American Motorcyclist, *June 1996*

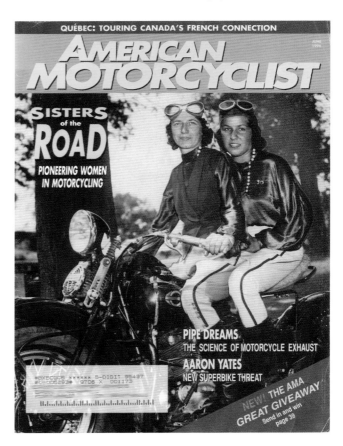

QUÉBEC: TOURING CANADA'S FRENCH CONNECTION

AMERICAN MOTORCYCLIST

SISTERS of the ROAD
PIONEERING WOMEN IN MOTORCYCLING

PIPE DREAMS
THE SCIENCE OF MOTORCYCLE EXHAUST

AARON YATES
NEW SUPERBIKE THREAT

NEW! THE AMA GREAT GIVEAWAY
Send in and win page 39

Nellie Jo Gill

Nellie Jo Gill, Lily Farrow's sister, lived in Columbus, Indiana. She too was in love with motorcycles and rode for many years in the 1930s and 1940s.

She was an avid bowler and rode hundreds of miles to play in tournaments. In 1941, Nellie Jo and her passenger, friend Eleanor Stanton, rode across the country to California to attend a Hollywood bowling tournament. According to the story she piloted her motorcycle right into the bowling alley.

Nellie Jo was an active member of the Motor Maids and attended many of their events. She was also a member of the Army Air Corps, retiring as a sergeant.

1931
Nellie Jo Gill on her Harley-Davidson.
Jane Farrow Langley

Circa 1945
Nellie Jo Gill, Arizona.
A. D. Farrow Co.

Circa 1945
Nellie Jo Gill,
New Mexico.
A. D. Farrow Co.

Circa late 1940s
Dorothy Farrow, wife of Don Farrow, was Lily's daughter-in-law, another of the Farrow
motorcycling clan. Here she is with friends out for a ride (left to right) Dorothy Farrow,
Carolyn Shop and Jackie Rhoades, Columbus, Ohio.

Charles R. Moor Photography, Columbus, Ohio

Alice Brady *1920s*

Another beautiful Wall of Death Rider in the 1920s was Alice Brady Merrill. He real name was Alice Treadwell from Kansasville, Wisconsin. She was married to Speedy (Merrill) Treadwell.

Alice was also a talented water show stunt diver, but performed mostly as a motordrome rider beginning in 1925. After a long illness, Alice passed away at an early age on February 3, 1930.

Simmons Family Collection

Alice Brady "The Mile-A-Minute Girl"

Mother and Daughter on a Comet *Circa 1920s*

Mom and darling daughter aboard *Comet*, their aptly named circa 1920 Harley-Davidson.

Simmons Family Collection

Olive Hager *1914 and on*

Born in Nashville, Tennessee in 1889, Olive Hager and her older brother Oliver had an ordinary life on the family farm. But Olive's life would be anything but ordinary. Olive's fascination with wheels started at an early age, and as a young girl she became the first female to drive an automobile in Nashville. She would become one of the first and most famous Wall of Death Riders of all time. Others used the name after her, but Olive was truly the first "Mile-a-Minute-Girl".

As the story is told, Olive began riding motorcycles with her brother Oliver K. Hager in about 1911. By 1914 the pair would be riding the dangerous "Wall of Death". Oliver, nicknamed *O.K.*, was three years older than Olive, and quite an accomplished trick rider himself. Olive was an adventurous girl and a fast learner, eventually becoming one of the only women to headline her own Wall of Death show. Olive and Oliver would ride their Indian motorcycles up and down the 16-foot perpendicular walls with reckless abandon, crisscrossing at high speeds to the very top of the high banks only to shoot suddenly to the bottom of the 38-foot in diameter enclosure. These daring feats caused chills up and down the spines of the astonished spectators who lined the top of the rails of the motordrome to watch.

When asked how she did it, Olive said, "It's easy when you know how. Anybody who understands the laws of gravitation knows how it's done. Unless a tire bursts, or there is a flaw in the machines, all one has to do is to steer straight ahead".

The brother and sister toured extensively throughout the teens, twenties and through the late thirties. Olive had other male riding partners that came and went. Bobby Gold was one that stayed for more than a season. Another well-known rider to join the act was Dudley "Daredevil" Lewis, whom Olive fell in love with and eventually married. They all rode together for several years, adding a second woman rider, Mrs. Bobby Gold, rounding out the foursome. Together they toured as part of the Sheesley Shows circuit from 1916 through the early 1920s, and later with the Johnny Jones exposition show in the late 1920s, and with other traveling shows.

In 1929, Fay Radcliff was another rider who would appear with Olive. The two worked beautifully together, riding at speeds from sixty to 100 miles per hour. Often, they would speed in opposite directions, barely missing each other, which was extremely dangerous.

"Dutch", as Olive was known to her friends, suffered many injuries over the years she challenged the wall—none of which stopped her. Her first serious accident came in 1916, when she collided with her brother and broke her pelvis, keeping her in bed for ten weeks.

Tragedy struck in 1918 when she was performing a stunt with another woman rider when the two struck head on while crisscrossing on the wall. The other girl was killed instantly while Olive lay unconscious for forty-eight hours with a concussion and four broken ribs. A few years later, in 1920 riding at a fair in Red Geer, Alberta, Canada, a tire on her motorcycle blew up, forcing Olive, at high speed, into a cable and leaving a severe gash on her right arm that required forty-eight stitches to close. In 1923 at the Texas Cotton Palace, Olive fell and broke her left arm while riding cross-legged on her machine.

There were many more spills and thrills for Olive, but she kept right on riding. There are records of her riding the wall well into the late 1930s. She often did interviews before her shows, putting down her favorite crossword puzzle to answer questions from inquisitive reporters, who were, no doubt, astonished that a daredevil stuntrider could be interested in as mundane an activity as working a crossword puzzle.

Away from the lights of the midway and the roar of the engines, Olive was a quiet, home loving woman, who loved domesticity and rode to fame because it was her profession. She confessed she loved the crowds and the noise and bustle of show life, but much preferred her farm in Vermont after the season had closed and tents were all folded away. But every spring, she'd head out on the road once again, thrilling crowds across the country.

Circa 1914
Down on the farm in Nashville, Tennessee. Olive and four friends pose on motorcycles. Second from left is a very rare 1914 Hendee Special, the first motorcycle with an electric starter.

Circa 1916
No-handed on the wall.
both photos, Simmons Family Collection

1927
Group shot taken in front of Hager's Wall of Death.

all photos, Simmons Family Collection

1937
Olive's Wall of Death/Lady Trick Rider Show.

Rare envelope from Hager's Wall of Death.

Circa 1920
Olive poses on her Indian motorcycle for publicity stills.

Circa 1920
Another pose for publicity stills. Note the bandage on her right arm after her fall in Canada left her with forty-eight stitches.

Circa 1923
Original page from Olive Hager's scrapbook.

1926 Olive and Dudley.

Mickey Apple *1920s*

In June of 1921, a pretty Wisconsin girl named Emma Louise Pakonian attended a motordrome show in Wausau. There, Mickey, as she was known, met Thurston James Apple, a daredevil rider, racer, and motordrome performer. They married after a whirlwind courtship. Mickey had never been on a motorcycle before, but she learned quickly, and joined her husband, performing in their motordrome show until its sale in 1947.

Circa 1930s
Mickey Apple sitting on her bike in a rare still moment, in front of the Apple Motordrome.

Key Nerland

Mickey Rides the Drome *Circa 1940s*
Mickey Apple and partner in action, riding the wall.

Key Nerland

1944
Mickey Apple on her Indian Scout.

Key Nerland

137

Two on a Cleveland *1921*
Why don't more ladies ride motorcycles?
MotorCycling and Bicycling, *March 16, 1921*

WHY DON'T MORE LADIES RIDE MOTORCYCLES?
Some day they will, but just now they are waiting for somebody to set the fashion, repeating bicycling history 20 years ago

Indian Rider *1921*
Unknown Indian rider shows that neatness counts. It was important for many early women riders to keep up their ladylike appearances while enjoying the sport.

MotorCycling and Bicycling, *March 16, 1921*

Did you see Mrs. Clymer–

at the Rochester Rally, riding her INDIAN Scout?

The ease and grace with which she handled it proved that the

Indian Scout is different

Powerful enough for a motor cop—and light enough for a girl to ride.

and the price now is

$250

—the Universal Motorcycle with the Universal Appeal

Hendee Manufacturing Co.
Largest Motorcycle Manufacturer in the World

Springfield, Mass.   U. S. A.

Indian Scout Ad *1922*
Advertisement for new Indian Scout featuring Mrs. Floyd Clymer, wife of well known motorcycle industry entrepreneur Floyd Clymer. Mrs. Clymer was a motorcycle enthusiast as well and was often seen piloting her own machine.

MotorCycling and Bicycling, *August 30, 1922*

Maud M. Randall *1922*

A well-known equestrienne from Atlanta, Maud M. Randall owned a large stable of horses where she taught many of Atlanta's young society women to ride—horses, that is. Maude purchased an Indian motorcycle and sidecar which she drove to Providence, Rhode Island, her former home. Later she returned to Atlanta and introduced the sport of motorcycling to young women. Maud is shown here with her two prize-winning French bulldogs, Frenchie and Buster.

MotorCycling and Bicycling *November 29, 1922*

Mrs. Clark, Chicago Gypsy *1922*

Mrs. Clark, of the Chicago Motorcycle Club, and friend, on the
Chicago Club's Gypsy Tour to Michigan City, Indiana.

MotorCycling and Bicycling, *June 28, 1922*

TO BE SEEN AT THE SHOW—THE EVANS POWER CYCLE

Snapped in beautiful Rochester, N. Y.

A motorcycle for the masses, low-priced, no cost for up-keep,
just the thing for errands around town or excursions into the
country, over a hundred miles to the gallon of gasoline

Ner-A-Car Ad *1922*

An advertisement for the
economical and easy to
ride Ner-A-Car. At $225, and
traveling 300 miles on a dollar's
worth of gas, it was cheap, fun
transportation.

MotorCycling and Bicycling,
June 28, 1922

Evans Power Cycle *1922*

Often called one of the finest American lightweights ever
built, the Evans Power Cycle was made from 1919-1924. It
got an amazing 100 miles to a gallon of gas.

Motorcycling in the Bicycling World, *January 23, 1924*

Lillian LaFrance *1924*

Lillian LaFrance was born Agnes Micek in Atwood, Kansas in 1894. Brought up on a farm, she was the second oldest of a family of twelve children and raised as a strict Catholic. In 1916, Agnes went to see the traveling carnival—an event that would change her life forever. In 1924, she began riding the wall of death and changed her name to the more marquis-worthy Lillian LaFrance.

These are her words, written in her journal from Rangoon (then in Burma, now Myanmar) on April 22, 1933: "At an early age I had the spirit of wanderlust, my desire for travel was Westward and the open spaces, and not to the big cities. Ever since 16, I was eager to do something to attain fame. I joined a carnival show and toured the States with them as 'The spider with a beautiful girl's head'".

"I really commenced my drome riding in 1924. My first lessons were with a small, specially constructed auto, using the engine of a 'Red Indian' motorcycle."

Lillian goes on to explain why she quit the show at the age of thirty-nine. Her last ride was in Toungoo, Burma:

"To the adventurous girl, and others who wish to lead a life of thrills and excitement like mine, I would like to show you the other side of the picture. A 'rolling stone gathers no moss'- in OUR life it should read- 'In a life of constant movements, you cannot make any firm friendships.' You can only see the other side of the picture as you get older. Then you will realize your loss. You have no home to go to, no children to lean on. You have given away the best years of your life chasing 'Willow-of-the-Wisps' of fame, and your declining years are spent without one true friend".

After her retirement from the carnival and the Wall of Death, Lillian found the roots she had longed for. She married Neil Hampton, the general agent for the Wortham shows, and with the birth of a son, Karl, Lillian had the family she always wanted. Leaving her globetrotting past behind her, she lived in Arizona for the remainder of her life and passed away in 1979 at the age of eighty-five.

Circa 1920s
Lillian with a friend.

Lily LaFrance, ready to ride.

Elks Midwinter Carnival, Honolulu *Circa 1920s*
Taken in Honolulu, Hawaii in the late 1920s as Lillian performed there for the Elks Midwinter Carnival.

All photos *Simmons Family Collection*

Ruth Robinson *1924*
Ruth Robinson, daughter of Jack Robinson,
Henderson dealer in Peoria, Illinois, demonstrated
Henderson motorcycles for her dad.

Motorcycling in the Bicycling World, May 28, 1924

Margaret Flynn *1925*
Margaret Flynn of Pittsfield, Massachusetts was the first
woman to purchase an Indian Prince. The single cylinder
machine was introduced in September of 1924.

Indian News #1, 1925

Fannie Peterson *Circa 1926*
Fannie Nichols Peterson was the wife of motorcycle dealer L.A.T. (Lawrence) Peterson
of Waterbury, Connecticut. L.A.T. was one of the first motorcycle dealers in the area
dating back to the mid 1900s. Fannie Peterson on her Indian Chief. The woman in the
sidecar may be her mother Anna Nichols.

Esta Manthos Indian Motorcycle Collection, Museum of Springfield History, Springfield,
Massachusetts

Velma Parrott *1925*

Velma Parrott, of Oakland, California, was one of the best known riders on the Pacific Coast. She rode Indians for a number of years. Here A. B. Lilenthal, a traffic cop, is trying to sell Miss Parrott a ticket to the Oakland Police Ball, but he finally wound up taking her to the ball himself.

Indian News # 1, 1925

Diamond Chain Ad *1925*

You can see why it's the champ.

Motorcycling, July 21, 1926

Step out with the "Champ"
and you'll never have to walk home

Diamond "449" the "heavyweight champion of motorcycle chains" will bring you home, no matter what you get into. Whether you're out for a view of the country from the finest of paved roads or whether you're on an errand through a rocky detour, **"449"**

Diamond "449" has the strength and stamina to pull you through.

Ask your dealer to show you "449." You can see why it's the "Champ."

"Heavy-weight" Champion of Motorcycle Chains

DIAMOND CHAIN & MFG. CO. Indianapolis, U.S.A.

Makers of High Grade Chains Since 1890

Mrs. Carl Doll *1925*

Mrs. Carl Doll, 95-pound bride of Carl Doll of the Mattman Sinclair Company, accompanied her husband on a 5,000 mile trip throughout the East, inspecting filling stations for his firm. The Dolls used an Indian Scout and sidevan. Mr. and Mrs. Doll took turns driving the rig.

Motorcycling and Bicycling World, February 4, 1925

Muriel Borek *1926*

The very photogenic Muriel Borek was a model Indian Motorcycle Co. used in their advertising campaign in 1926. She graces the cover of the October/November 1926 *Indian News* and appears in several of their ads during that time.

Muriel on the cover of the Indian News, October/ November 1926.

Indian News, *October/November 1926.*

Muriel and unidentified passenger.

American Motorcycling and Bicycling, *November, 1926*

Mrs. Seth Davidson *1926*
Showing that Mount Hood's snow held no terrors for Portland's fair motorcyclists, Mrs. Seth Davidson and her friend, Mrs. Wells Bennett (standing) frequently tackled the snowy pass on this Henderson 4-cylinder with sidecar, circa 1925. Both intrepid riders believed that a motorcycle was the only way to truly enjoy the natural beauty of Oregon.

MotorCycle & Bicycle Illustrated, *March 31, 1926*

Bessie Warren *1928*
Bessie Warren of Kansas City, Missouri, was an expert at handling Indians.

Indian News, *June 1928*

Dot Robinson

What hasn't been written or said about this five-foot-two, redheaded dynamo on the pink motorcycle? Dot has done more single-handedly to promote women in motorcycling than anyone before or since. She set the bar and paved the way, always a lady.

Born in Melbourne, Australia in 1912, Dot was the daughter of Jim Goulding, maker of the Goulding sidecar. So naturally, Dot's motorcycling habit began in a sidecar when she was only three years old. The family moved to Michigan when she was eleven, and her father opened a Harley-Davidson dealership in Saginaw. Dot worked as a bookkeeper when she was just a teenager and bought her first motorcycle when she was sixteen.

In 1930, Dot won her first trophy in the Flint 100 Enduro Men's Sidecar class. She most always competed against men, as there were no women's class events until the 1960s. During the 1930s, Dot won or placed in over fifty endurance runs. One of Dot's favorite wins was a nineteen-hour Thanksgiving Day event in Columbus, Ohio. Dot was the only female entrant. With her father in the sidecar, Dot won with a score 100 points higher than the second place finisher.

While working in the shop, Dot met Earl Robinson, a customer and fellow motorcycle enthusiast. They were married in 1931, and continued their life of motorcycles and more motorcycles. Daughter Betty was brought up riding in a sidecar, often accompanying Dot on her travels around the country. Eventually, Betty also became an accomplished rider. She too started riding at an early age, and when she was sixteen Betty and Dot embarked on an 11,000 mile trip across the United States. Dot and Betty would become motorcycling's most famous mother-daughter duo.

Dot competed successfully, mostly against men, in sidecar competitions and endurance races from the 1930s through 1960. Among her notable accomplishments were earning a perfect score in a one hundred mile endurance race, and finished second in the two-day 1937 Jack Pine Enduro. She came back to the Enduro to take first in 1940.

Dot and Earl, a well-known motorcyclist in his own right, set a new sidecar record in 1935 for a transcontinental crossing on their trusty Harley-Davidson '74 with Goulding sidecar. They traveled from Los Angeles to New York in an unbelievable time of eighty-nine hours, fifty-eight minutes. The pair covered the 1,000 miles in twenty-four hours, though there were periods of heavy rain and hazardous washed-out roads. They started out riding 100 miles relays each at night, and a half-day each in the daytime. The sidecar was stocked with food, so they did not have to stop for meals. While one drove, the other could stretch out and sleep in the sidecar. The pair rode the last forty-eight hours entirely in the rain. It was said that Dot did most of the driving and fought the bulk of the elements; Earl was feeling a little under the weather for the majority of the trip.

In 1939 Dot acted on a great idea given to her by friend and fellow motorcyclist Linda Dugeau—a nationwide club for women riders. She traveled all over the United States looking for women who owned and rode their own motorcycles. By 1941, she had assembled the fifty-one charter members of a new group called The Motor Maids. Dot became the first president of the Motor Maids, a position she would hold for over twenty-five years.

Dot and Earl opened their own Harley-Davidson dealership in 1935, which they ran until 1971. In 1979, the husband and wife team were awarded the prestigious A.M.A. Dud Perkins Award.

Without a doubt, Dot was the definitive First Lady of Motorcycling, racking up well over one-and-a-half million miles on her thirty-five Harley-Davidsons. She continued to ride until the age of eighty-five and was inducted into the A.M.A.'s Motorcycle Hall of Fame in 1998. She passed away in 1999 at the end of her life's rich, exciting journey. Dot Robinson's legacy continues—her name will always be synonymous with women and motorcycling.

1929
Dot Robinson at seventeen in the Arthur High School Parade.

Betty Robinson Fauls

1935
Dot and husband Earl with the bike they rode to set the Transcontinental Record in 1935.

Betty Robinson Fauls

1938
Dot Robinson's seven-year-old daughter
Betty with a special Christmas gift—a sidecar
made by grandfather Jimmy Goulding.

Betty Robinson Fauls

1937
"First Lady of Motorcycling" Dot Robinson on her 1937 Harley-Davidson '45.

Betty Robinson Fauls

1939
Dot and Betty at Laconia, New Hampshire in 1939.
National Motorcycle Museum, Anamosa, Iowa

1941
On a trip from their home near Detroit, Michigan, Dot and nine-year-old Betty Jane arrive in Laconia, New Hampshire.
Betty Robinson Fauls

1946
Dot and her sidecar passenger pushing through
the mud in a 1946 Endurance Run.

Betty Robinson Fauls

Circa 1946
Dot and Betty, the ultimate mother-
daughter motorcycle team in matching
Motor Maids uniforms, right down to the
names on their hats.

Betty Robinson Fauls

1950
Beautiful May, 1950 *Motorcyclist*
magazine cover featuring the art
of the great Fredrickson Day.

Motorcyclist, *May 1950*

Indian News
1928
Gorgeous cover featuring a charming unknown rider.
Indian News,
April/May 1928

Viola Pelaquin *1928*

Daring, adorable Viola of the famous Pelaquin motordrome family of wall of death riders in a rare still moment. Viola rode the wall with her husband Joe until she had her first child in 1929. Later, her sons Joe Junior, Sonny, Frankie and Russell would keep up the tradition and become great wall riders too.

The Pelaquin Family

Vivian Bales *1929*

A beautiful, seventeen-year-old, 95 pound, 5 foot 2 inch dance teacher from Georgia, Vivian Bales bought herself a Harley-Davidson and taught herself how to ride in 1926. In love with motorcycling and filled with a sense of adventure, Vivian wrote a letter to Harley-Davidson in 1929 describing her plans to ride from Georgia to Milwaukee. She intended to visit Harley-Davison dealers along the route. The trip ended up to be close to 5,000 miles when she was done.

The factory realized that a pretty woman rider could be great for publicity and they dubbed Vivian, "The Enthusiast Girl". In the summer of 1929 it took her seventy-eight days to make the loop up through Georgia, the Midwest and into Milwaukee to the Harley factory. In many of the towns she visited, Vivian was greeted by local dignitaries, who would often roll out the red carpet for her.

One of her greatest thrills was meeting President Hoover, which she describes in great detail in one of the articles about her journey that was printed in an issue of Harley-Davidson's Enthusiast magazine.

A favorite excerpt: "Officer Jack Spencer escorted me to South Haven. We rolled in at twilight. On the way over we unwound the throttles and my little ol' '45 moved the speedometer hand to the number 85. I ran away from Officer Jack! I shouldn't tell that, I suppose. Officer Jack is a gentleman. For the girls that read this, I want to confess that I hated to leave lots of places, to part with many good fellows. You know how it is".

Vivian continued motorcycling after her *Enthusiast Girl* days. She performed stunt riding at motorcycle races in Tallahassee, Florida. She never bought another motorcycle, but Vivian said that her Harley-Davidson experience was one of the most significant of her life.

Before she passed away on December 23, 2001, only three weeks before her ninety-third birthday, Vivian asked for a motorcycle procession at her funeral. Her request was granted, and organized through Flint River Harley-Davidson of Albany. For the Georgia Peach, this was a fitting final expression.

OPPOSITE: Vivian Bales, *The Enthusiast Girl* poses on her Harley-Davidson with the trophy and sweater she got from Harley-Davidson.
Harley-Davidson Archives, copyright H-D

Vivian on the cover of *The Harley-Davidson Enthusiast*, May 1929. (She would also appear again on the cover of the November 1929 issue.)

Harley-Davidson Archives, copyright H-D

1930 to 1939

OPPOSITE: 1939 Cartoon

"The riding lesson"

Motorcyclist, *February 1938*

Indian Fans of All Ages *Circa 1930s*

A group of female Indian riders pose in front of the local Indian dealership. Even the cute little girl in the front is ready to hit the open road.

Simmons Family Collection

Kathleen Rose *1930*
Kathleen Rose on her white Indian. She was a member of the
San Francisco Motorcycle Club.

Indian News, *June 1930*

Mabel Roop *1930*
Daring Mabel Roop rode a 37 cubic-inch Indian Scout. Her father
and brother rode Indians too.

Indian News, *June 1930*

Mrs. Roland Free *1930*
Mrs. Roland Free, wife of the Indian representative in Indianapolis,
Indiana, with Mrs. Charles Clements both Indian enthusiasts.

Indian News, *June 1930*

Above is shown Majorie (Margie) Kemp, a featured rider with Dare-Devil Kemp's Motordrome with the World at Home Shows. The picture was taken on the ground immediately in front of the ballyhoo platform of the 'drome.

Circa 1930s
Newspaper clipping: Marjorie makes the news.
Simmons Family Collection

Marjorie Kemp *Circa 1930s*

One of the more well known women Wall of Death riders and from a Motordrome family, Marjorie Kemp often headlined her own motordrome show featuring all girl riders. She was a featured rider with the Dare-Devil Kemp's Motordrome with the World at Home Shows and one of the stars of the Royal American Shows as well.

Marjorie called her troupe the "Legion of Mad Speed Demons" as she raced around motordromes at seventy miles per hour, often trading her Excelsior motorcycle for a car with her pet lion Nero riding beside her. In 1933, she suffered a bitten shoulder when one of the lions fell out of one of the automobiles used in the act.

Marjorie's show played at the 1934 Chicago World's Fair, where for twenty-six weeks she rode with the 400-pound Nubian-bred lion, defying death by roaring around the wall of the motordrome.

Circa 1930s
An interview with Marjorie.
Simmons Family Collection

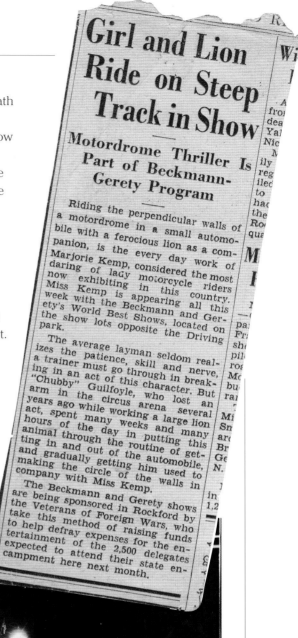

Girl and Lion Ride on Steep Track in Show

Motordrome Thriller Is Part of Beckmann-Gerety Program

Riding the perpendicular walls of a motordrome in a small automobile with a ferocious lion as a companion, is the every day work of Marjorie Kemp, considered the most daring of lady motorcycle riders now exhibiting in this country. Miss Kemp is appearing all this week with the Beckmann and Gerety's World Best Shows, located on the show lots opposite the Driving park.

The average layman seldom realizes the patience, skill and nerve, a trainer must go through in breaking in an act of this character. But "Chubby" Guilfoyle, who lost an arm in the circus arena several years ago while working a large lion act, spent many weeks and many hours of the day in putting this animal through the routine of getting in and out of the automobile, and gradually getting him used to making the circle of the walls in company with Miss Kemp.

The Beckmann and Gerety shows are being sponsored in Rockford by the Veterans of Foreign Wars, who take this method of raising funds to help defray expenses for the entertainment of the 2,500 delegates expected to attend their state encampment here next month.

Night riders *Circa 1930s*
Beautifully lit night shot of Kemp's Motor Stadium. Marjorie Kemp is the rider on the right. The girl on the left is unknown.

Simmons Family Collection

The Motorcyclist Inaugural Magazine Cover

1932

Cover November 1932 is the first issue of *The Motorcyclist*, which would become the official publication of the American Motorcyclist Association. Fittingly, it features a female Harley-Davidson rider.

Motorcyclist, *November 1932*

The MOTORCYCLIST

Official A.M.A. *Publication*

"HI FOLKS!"

. . . *November, Nineteen-Thirty-two* . . .

Orange County Girls *1930*
A handful of the female members of the Orange County Motorcycle Club from Santa Ana, California pose in their riding clothes.

Simmons Family Collection

OVERLEAF: Fair Riders' Hohokus, New Jersey *Circa early 1930s*
Pictured are riders who attended the Hohokus, New Jersey race.

Rose Vlatkin *New York City*
Josephine Maddi *Bayonne, New Jersey*
Ruth Hall *Brooklyn, New York*
Florence Taylor *Kerney, New Jersey*
Evelyn Currid *Newark, New Jersey*
Dorothy Rose *New York City*
Mrs. Dona Wiegand *Plainfield, New Jersey*
Mrs. Dorothy Meisel *Brooklyn, New York*
Mable Lake *Brooklyn, New York*

Simmons Family Collection

Helen Kiss *1930s*

Helen Kiss Main hailed from Pottstown, Pennsylvania. She was the daughter of Frank Kiss, the local Indian Motorcycle dealer. At 16 years of age, she was already riding an Indian Sport Scout and was a popular member of the Pottstown Roamer's Motorcycle Club. Helen later became a founding member of the Motor Maids, and served as its first Treasurer.

The adorable and photogenic Helen was known for her flashy riding outfits and matching paint jobs on her Indian motorcycles. She appeared in magazine ads for Duckworth Chains and others. She was known as "The Pink Lady" in the 1940s for her factory-painted pink motorcycle. No doubt, the eye-catching color helped her win the first Carol DuPont Award at the Laconia Meet for the best-dressed girl.

Helen won other awards over the years, including one in 1939 at the New England Gypsy Tour in Syracuse for neatest-dressed girl rider. Today Helen lives in Hampton, Virginia.

How would you like to get a new Indian Sport Scout for your birthday? That's what happened to Helen M. Kiss, daughter of Frank Kiss, Indian Dealer of Pottstown, Pa. Helen is Frank's youngest daughter, attends the Pottstown High School, is 16 years old and a member of the Pottstown Roamers Motorcycle Club.

Indian News, 1936,
Baer Family Library

Duckworth Chain Ad Featuring Helen Kiss.
Motorcyclist, April 1938

1939
Indian display model.
Baer Family Library

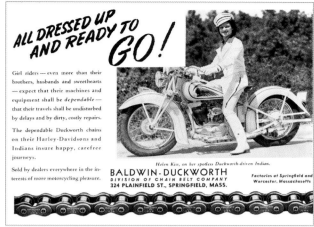

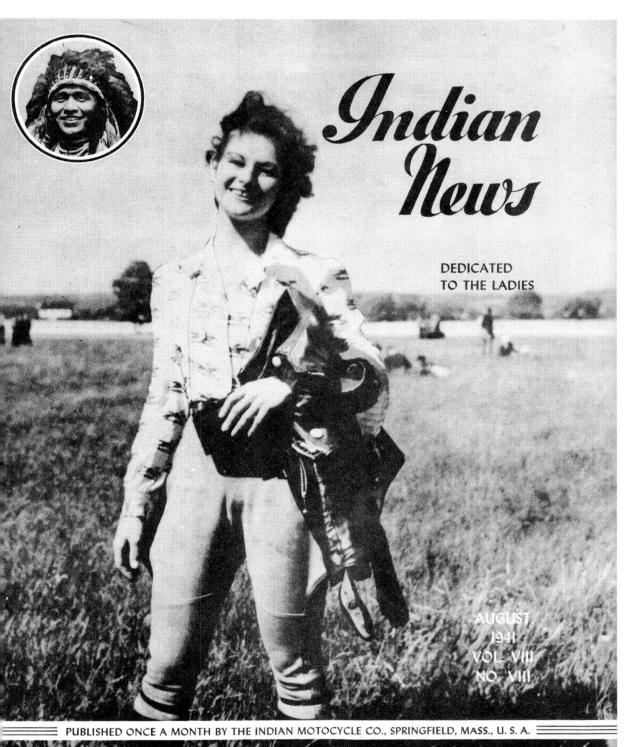

Left to right—Dot Smith, Helen Kiss and Mavis Gallan, all three prize winners at the rally

Motorcyclist, *July 1940*

Louise Scherbyn *1930s*

Born in Waterloo New York, Louise was a lifelong, die-hard Indian motorcycle lover. It all began with her husband George, who wanted to share his hobbies with his young wife. He tried to teach her to shoot, and she fell off a log. He took her fishing but she never caught anything. Then he put her on a motorcycle—and away she went. In 1933, she purchased her own motorcycle, a 1932 Indian Pony, and was hooked for life. Louise stored the motorcycle in her basement, devoured the factory Rider's Instruction Book and was riding solo after her third lesson.

Louise was probably the first woman motorcyclist in Rochester back in 1933. In 1937, she took her first solo trip to Chicago, a distance of 1,200 miles. Then, in 1938, in sub-zero weather, she headed south to the National Championships, riding a sidecar rig to Daytona Beach, some 2,800 miles away. Louise must have loved being a long-distance solo rider—in 1938 she completed a 900-mile solo ride through New England and the Adirondack mountains. On the entire trip, she used thirteen gallons of gasoline and four quarts of oil.

On a four-day, thousand-mile trip through Northern Canada in 1939, Louise visited the famous Dionne Quintuplets in Callander, Quebec.

In 1941, she made another lone trek—1,800 miles to Quebec and down through New England, stopping in Laconia, New Hampshire to attend the launching of the Motor Maids.

In 1940 and again in 1941, she staged and participated in the first and second All-Girl Motorcycle Show in Waterloo, New York, where she performed stunt riding to the amazement of the crowds.

Louise put a lot of miles on her Indians—but she also knew how to squeeze maximum mileage from a tank of gas. In 1941, Louise was awarded First Prize in the Waterloo Scotchman's Derby, going 103.2 miles on one gallon of gas.

Louise always loved Indian Motorcycles, and owned three of them over the years, all painted white. For over thirty years, she was not only a cross-country endurance rider and a celebrated stunt rider, but she rode in carnival motordromes and toured the United States and Canada. Louise was proud to say that she never had an accident on her bike while logging over 225,000 miles. Could it have been the lucky rabbit's foot she kept in her saddlebag?

In 1943, Louise served as associate editor and the only woman columnist of *Motorcyclist* magazine. She also served as National Secretary of the Motor Maids, and became known as one of the greatest women motorcyclists in the world. She was also a member of the Wa-Co-Mo-Pals, the all-girl motorcycle club of Newark, New Jersey.

In 1950, Louise founded the Women's International Motorcycle Association (W.I.M.A.), which in 2009 boasted over 3,000 members in twenty countries.

Louise gave up riding in the 1960s due to arthritis, but she continued to run and edit the WIMA newsletter well into the early 1980s. Louise passed away on June 18, 2003, with many wonderful miles behind her, and a remarkable life lived.

1940

Louise performing a motorcycle stunt on September 29, 1940 at the All-Girl Motorcycle Show, Waterloo, New York. Her trusting co-riders in the stunt are fellow members of the Wa-Co-Mo-Pals, Margaret Johnson and Pauline Groat.

Esta Manthos Indian Motorcycle Collection, Museum of Springfield History, Springfield, Massachusetts

1940

Poster advertising the first All Girls Show.

Esta Manthos Indian Motorcycle Collection, Museum of Springfield History, Springfield, Massachusetts

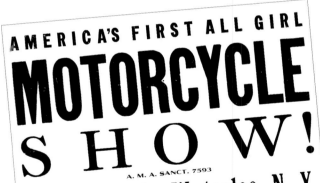

AMERICA'S FIRST ALL GIRL
MOTORCYCLE SHOW!
A. M. A. SANCT. 7593
Fair Grounds, Waterloo, N. Y.
Sunday, Sep. 29, 1940, at 1.30 P.M.
See New York State's All Girl Riders In Action
Admission 25c PLUS TAX
RAIN DATE — OCTOBER 6th
FREE PARKING
Auspices WA-CO-MO Pals of Newark, N. Y.

ALL GIRLS
MOTORCYCLE
SHOW!
A. M. A. SANCT. 8324

Fair Grounds, Waterloo, N.Y.

Sunday, August 3, 1941
At 2.00 P. M. D. S. T.

SEE AMERICA'S ALL GIRL RIDERS IN ACTION

FREE PARKING

Admission - 30c Tax Inc.

WA-CO-MO Pals Motorcycle Club

1941
Poster advertising the
second All Girls Show on
August 3, 1941.
Simmons Family Collection

1941
Louise Scherbyn on her second solo trip to
Quebec, Canada.
*Esta Manthos Indian Motorcycle Collection, Museum of
Springfield History, Springfield, Massachusetts*

1942
Louise on her trademark white Indian while
touring the Midwest.
*Esta Manthos Indian Motorcycle Collection, Museum of
Springfield History, Springfield, Massachusetts*

Bessie Stringfield *1930s*

Born in Kingston, Jamaica in 1911, Bessie Stringfield was an amazing woman on many levels. T*he tiny, spirited, African American "Motorcycle Queen of Miami" was* an inspiration and an icon.

Bessie certainly had a rough beginning. Her mother died in childbirth, and her father abandoned her at age five. She was soon adopted by a wealthy, Irish woman who encouraged her to follow her dreams and stand up for what she believed in. One of those dreams was to ride a motorcycle—and that she did!

At the early age of sixteen her first motorcycle was a 1928 Indian 101 Scout, which was followed by twenty-seven Harleys over a span of sixty-six years.

Bessie never let the prejudice of both gender and race stop her from enjoying her many years of riding. Before Rosa Parks ever got on that bus and before the Civil Rights Movement began, Bessie spent many nights sleeping on her motorcycle at gas stations after being turned away at hotels and motels.

Bessie always held her head high and kept a positive attitude throughout her life. Her accomplishments were enormous. The first

African-American woman to ride cross-country solo, she made the trip many times, often leaving home for months at a time. Bessie used what she called the "money method" to plan her trips. She would toss a penny over a map—and wherever it landed is where she would go. She rode extensively through all forty-eight contiguous states, Mexico, Canada and Hawaii.

During World War II, she joined the motorcycle dispatch—the only woman in her unit. From 1941 to 1945, Bessie traveled some of the country's roughest roads, delivering classified documents. Later, she rode in flat track races and in a carnival motordrome show. There wasn't much Bessie couldn't or didn't do on a motorcycle.

As she got older, Bessie suffered from an enlarged heart, but that didn't stop her either. Said Bessie, "Years ago the doctor wanted to stop me from riding. I told him if I don't ride, I won't live long. I never did quit."

In 1990, Bessie was finally honored as she deserved. At the age of seventy-nine she was honored at the opening of the Motorcycle Heritage Museum. Bessie remained active in motorcycling until she passed away in 1993.

Circa 1930
Young Bessie Stringfield in her riding cap.
Bessie Stringfield Collection

Motorcycle Queen of Miami

Besse Springfield Collection

Bessie Stringfield
Photo by Johnson of Miami, A.M.A. Archives

Barney Londerman and Hazel Bethel *1932*
Two expert riders from California, Barney Londerman, from Oakland, Hazel Bethel, from Merced.
    Motorcyclist, *December 1932*

Mrs. George W. Clifford *1932*
Mrs. Clifford, from Cedar Rapids, Iowa, was the only woman rider "in those parts." She inspired many other women to get interested in the sport.
    Motorcyclist, *November 1932*

Ann Clark—*Miss Ambition* 1933

Ann Clark was elected secretary of the Keystone Erie Motorcycle Club of Erie, Pennsylvania. The local motorcycle dealer dubbed her *Miss Ambition* because of all the hard work she put into planning motorcycle events for the club. Here, she's ready to ride no matter what Mother Nature dishes out in a one piece, rough weather outfit.

Motorcyclist, *March 1933*

Hazel and the Mojave 1933

Hazel Bethel, from Merced, California had been riding her Indian Scout for over two years when she decided to take a solo trip to see her sister, who lived in Oklahoma City.

Hazel headed out across the Mojave Desert, riding over 515 miles that first day in only twelve hours. She made her way over the punishing, dry desert roads with blistering temperatures reaching up to 122 degrees.

The total mileage for the trip was 4,808 miles round trip. Along the way she suffered two flat tires and had a minor fall on a newly graveled road. But all in all, Hazel's Indian admirably withstood the worst the desert could dish out, averaging sixty-one miles per gallon and 500 miles per quart of oil.

Motorcyclist, *October 1933*

Mrs. Crede Buchanan

1933

Portland, Oregon Indian fan Mrs. Crede Buchanan looks good on her Indian motorcycle.

Motorcyclist, *January 1933*

Harley-Davidson VL Rider *1934*

Unknown girl rider on a popular 1934 Harley-Davidson VL.

Alex Blendl Collection

Southern California Race *1933*
Women line up at a Southern California race event. Taken on July 23, 1933.
Photo by Churchill Gardiner Studio. Simmons Family Collection

Dotty Herbert *1935*
Dotty Herbert, the great
equestrienne of Ringling
Brothers and Barnum
Bailey Combined Show,
enthusiastically considers the
possibilities of an Indian Sport
Scout.

*Esta Manthos Indian Motorcycle
Collection, Museum of Springfield
History, Springfield, Massachusetts*

Florence Burnham *1936*
Florence, an outboard and
motorcycle racing champ and
cyclist of Wilmington, Delaware
sports a new Harley-Davidson
'61, which is resplendent in
white and chrome.

Motorcyclist, *June 1936*

HARLEY-DAVIDSON
Enthusiast

MAY 1936
FIVE CENTS

Enthusiast **Magazine Cover**
1936
Mrs. Preston Wilson, wife of the Hackensack, New Jersey Harley-Davidson dealer, arrives opening day, April 15, 1936, at Old Tappan, a favorite spot on the Hackensack River. Her catch that day were two brown trout, seventeen and nineteen inches.

Photo by W.T. Skinner, Harley-Davidson Archives, copyright H-D

Miss Polly Forbes-Johnson on her Indian Scout.

MANHATTAN

TO MEXICO

19-year-old Bennington College student takes 6,000-mile motorcycle tour.

Polly Forbes-Johnson, Bennington (Vt.) College Student—Makes 6,000-Mile Solo Tour

"I got a motorcycle in April last year", Miss Johnson said, "and this Spring I decided to make a trip down into Central America to see the country and the people."

Just like that — Miss Polly Forbes-Johnson took her Indian Scout, a sleeping roll, a pair of saddle bags and money enough for food and gas—and set off alone on her 6,000 mile trip that eventually led her from the skyscrapers of lower Manhattan thru the United States to Texas, then into Mexico and thru some of the wildest country man or woman ever traversed.

She slept in Indian huts, general stores, a post office, ranch houses, hay lofts.

She had no trouble at all in the "States" but things commenced to be different across the border—since she could not speak a word of Mexican—she gestured.

Getting into the "rough" after leaving Mexico City behind, Miss Johnson rammed the crankcase of her machine over a boulder—her ingenuity saved the day—taking a cake of soap from her saddle bag, she filled the crack with soap—it held—for a while. For two days she rode along, stopping periodically to renew the filling of the cracked case. At a village smittys stand—Polly gestured some more—crossed her fingers—and watched in amusement the blacksmith repair the damage.

Four days later she arrived at Guatemala City—her reputation traveled faster than she did—and she was met by Mr. Sanchos La-Tour—head of the city's tourist association.

Still gesturing and amusedly awaiting the outcome, she was introduced to President Ubico. The President—a motorcycle fan himself—listened with awe to her adventures and in return presented her with a brand new motorcycle as a souvenir of her visit with him.

Miss Polly, nearing the end of her time limit—happily boarded the Grace Liner, Santa Rosa, and sailed away to New York City where her reputation again beat her to the count—she was welcomed home by her mother and press officials.

Miss Polly—formerly of Bennington (Vt.) College is now staying in New York City with her mother to study photography.

Polly Forbes-Johnson *1936*

Tale of the adventure of Polly Forbes-Johnson on her trip from New York to Mexico.

Indian News, *December 1936*

Uncle Ole's Farm *1937*

Unknown motorcyclist, taken at "Uncle Ole's Farm", Dodgeville Wisconsin, August 8, 1937.

Simmons Family Collection

Riders and Picnickers *1937*

Two unknown riders from the 1937 Jack Pine Gypsy Picnic.

Carl Edeburn

Florence Emde *1937*

Florence Gavett, later to become Florence Emde, got involved in motorcycling in San Diego, California, encouraged by her brother Jack, an avid motorcyclist. She eventually met local racing star Floyd Emde at an event, and before long the two were married. With Florence's support, Floyd went on to win numerous local, state and National Championship races in his career, including the prestigious Daytona 200 road race.

Following Floyd's racing career, he and Florence opened first one, then two motorcycle retail stores in the San Diego area. Floyd oversaw the Sales and Service end of the business, while Florence kept the books. The two built a successful thirty-five year business in the San Diego area. Floyd and Florence had five children, four of whom raced motorcycles. When son Don Emde won the 1972 Daytona 200, Florence gained the distinction of becoming the wife of one Daytona 200 winner, and the mother of another. Floyd Emde passed away in 1994, while Florence lives today in Escondido, just north of downtown San Diego.

Don Emde Collection

Marge Halden *1938*
Marge Halden, member of the Fresno, California
Motorcycle Club proudly astride her ride.
Motorcyclist, *August, 1938*

Genevieve "Gyp" Baker *1938*
On May 15, 1938, Harry's Roamers held their
500-mile endurance run. At 4:00 a.m., twenty-five
riders lined up for the start of the race, including
the club's only lady rider, Genevieve "Gyp" Baker.
A cold wind blew across the sand and gravel road,
dotted with detours and dust. Later in the day,
a pounding rain pelted the riders. Twelve hours
and forty-five minutes later the first rider crossed
the finish line. That rider was "Gyp" Baker on her
Indian Sport Scout.

Later that year on New Year's Eve, "Gyp" set
another record, riding her motorcycle in sub-zero
weather, on icy roads and through deep snow to
summit Pike's Peak.
Motorcyclist, *June, 1938*

Mary Walker *1939*

Mary "Johnnie" Walker was born in Oklahoma and moved to Bakersfield, California when she was a teenager. She grew up with brothers and since they rode motorcycles, she did too. She learned to ride when she was seventeen. Her best girlfriend was also named Mary, so her uncle nicknamed her Johnnie.

Mary rode for five or six years before she got married and started having kids. Her daughter Cindy also became a rider years later. Today eighty-eight year old Mary Walker lives in Southern California.

1938
Portrait of Mary wearing her motorcycle goggles.
The Walker Family

1939
With her Indian motorcycle in late 1930s.
The Walker Family

1940
Mary, wearing a hat and a smile, sits on a bike talking to her brother's girlfriend (who is wearing goggles) at a hill-climb outside of Bakersfield.
The Walker Family

The Sacramento Cyclettes *1938*
Organized by twelve girls whose object was to be entirely independent, the Sacramento Cyclettes organization was not an auxiliary to any other club, but would work with any other club when asked. In six months, they had thirty members in good standing.

Motorcyclist, *February 1938*

Vivian Nelson *1938*
Daring circus trapeze performer Vivian Nelson balances atop a circa 1936 Indian Four. This particular, short lived Model 436 was made with the exhaust over intake, making it known as the "Upside Down Four". Only about 1,600 of these motorcycles were completed in the two years it in production in 1936 and 1937.

Motorcyclist, *June 1938*

San Francisco Motorcycle Club *1938*
Some of the members of the San Francisco
Motorcycle Club Auxiliary showing off their
attractive riding uniforms. The banner honors the
first crossing of the Golden Gate Bridge.

Motorcyclist, *February 1938*

Scotty Woodson *1938*
Scotty Woodson, winner of the best-dressed girl
contest at the Southern California rally. "The
feminine contingent in motorcycling contributed
much to uniform ideas and this is a fair illustration
of what the girls can do when they combine ideas
of design and riding". Scotty rode her own machine.

Motorcyclist, *October 1938*

**1939 Diamond
Chain Ad**
Advertisement for
Diamond Chain,
featuring a Harley-
Davidson rider.
Motorcyclist,
June 1939

MORE MILES FEWER ADJUSTMENTS

TRADE ◆ MARK

The "Diamond" on the links
is for your protection

The Improved MOTORCYCLE CHAIN ◆

Made with the precision of a roller bearing—the new improved Diamond Motorcycle Chain is stronger and lighter than ever before...No"wearing-in" period is necessary—wear is evenly distributed to prolong life, transmit all the power and add to the speed and joy of motorcycling.

Put the New Diamond Chain on your mount and note the difference.

DIAMOND CHAIN & MFG. CO.

469 Kentucky Avenue   Indianapolis, Indiana

Offices and Distributors in Principal Cities

DIAMOND
MOTORCYCLE CHAIN

HIT OF THE HIGHWAY

★ Wherever you go—tour, climb, Tourist Trophy or race—you'll see the top flight riders on Firestone Triple-Safe Tires. They choose Firestone for the extra safety and protection that only Firestone's patented construction features provide. The patented Gum-Dipped Cord Body gives greater protection against blowouts, two extra layers of Gum-Dipped Cords under the tread provide added protection against punctures, and the famous Firestone Tread design grips the road firmly for quick stops and stiff layovers.

Start the busy riding season "tire-safe"—drive in to your nearest Firestone motorcycle dealer and equip with Firestone Triple-Safe Tires today.

See Firestone Tires made in the Firestone Factory and Exhibition Building at New York World's Fair. Also visit the Firestone Exhibit at the Golden Gate International Exposition at San Francisco.

Listen to the Voice of Firestone with Richard Crooks, Margaret Speaks and the Firestone Symphony Orchestra, under the direction of Alfred Wallenstein, Monday evenings, over Nationwide N. B. C. Red Network.

1939 Firestone Tire Ad

Motorcyclist, *June 1939*

Firestone
TRIPLE-SAFE
MOTORCYCLE TIRES

★ SPEEDWAY-PROVED FOR HIGHWAY SAFETY

★ SPECIFY FIRESTONES ON YOUR NEXT MOTORCYCLE

Unknown Rider on an Indian Prince *1938*

An unknown rider on an Indian Prince sporting knee socks and knickers.

Motorcyclist, *April 1938*

Lou Riggsby *1939*

Lou Riggsby, from Chattonoga, Tennessee (who became Vice-President of the Motor Maids in 1943) poses in a 1939 ad for the Baldwin-Duckworth Chain Corporation.

Motorcyclist, *June 1939*

Lou Riggsby, caught in an informal pose. Lou and her Indian are well known to race-goers throughout the Middle West and South.

To the Ladies..

If you ride, you are safer, surer, because your Indian or Harley-Davidson is equipped with Duckworth Chains. If your husband or sweetie is the rider, he has the same security for he's riding on Duckworth Chains, too. They are standard equipment on all American motorcycles. When replacement becomes necessary, you can always get genuine Duckworth Chains, for Dealers everywhere sell them.

BALDWIN-DUCKWORTH CHAIN CORPORATION
SPRINGFIELD, MASS.
FACTORIES AT SPRINGFIELD AND WORCESTER, MASS.

1939 Buckeye Motorcycle Club
Gathering of the 1939 Buckeye Girls Club, the
A.M.A. National Champions from Columbus, Ohio.

Jane Farrow Langley

1939 Cartoon
Motorcyclist, *June 1939*

OVERLEAF: 1939 Indian Double Page Ad
For their 1939 *Ladies Number* issue of *Motorcyclist*
magazine, Indian placed this wonderful two-page
ad, featuring women riders.

Motorcyclist, *June 1939*

GIRLS TAKE TO *Motorcycling* TOO..

Because:

Travel expenses are low...

It's easy to get thru traffic...

It takes one out into the open air...

It helps show one how to live enjoyably without lots of frills...

Since the announcement of the Indian Junior Scout—more and more girls have found that it's easy to ride a motorcycle.

Talk it over with the Indian Dealer—he'll be glad to explain how you can ride away on a new Indian by making only a small payment.

Indian MOTORCYCLES

If by chance, you do not know the Indian Motorcycle Dealer near you, just drop us a line —we'll be glad to tell you.

INDIAN MOTORCYCLE COMPANY
SPRINGFIELD, MASS., U.S.A.

A MOTORCYCL
THE SAFEST M

INDIAN RIDERS WIN AT RICHMOND RALLY AND GYPSY TOUR

RESULTS SPEAK FOR THEMSELVES

Time Trials

1.	Woodsie Castonguay	INDIAN	29:54*
2.	Freddy Toscani	INDIAN	29:93*
3.	Lester Hillbish	INDIAN	29:97*
4.	Dick Fox	INDIAN	30:13

1st 5-Mile Expert (5:09:00)**

1.	Woodsie Castonguay	INDIAN
2.	Lester Hillbish	INDIAN
3.	J. B. Jones	H-D

2nd 5-Mile Expert (5:09:08)

1.	Stanley Witinski	INDIAN
2.	Freddy Toscani	INDIAN
3.	Dick Fox	INDIAN

10-Mile Feature Race (10:19:00)**

1.	Woodsie Castonguay	INDIAN
2.	Benny Campanale	H-D
3.	Freddy Toscani	INDIAN
4.	Lester Hillbish	INDIAN

The winning of the 5-mile record again gives Indian every record on the half mile track.

*Three Indian Riders turned the ½-mile during Time Trials under 30 seconds for the FIRST TIME IN CLASS "C" HISTORY.

**New Records.

WHEN PROPERLY HANDLED, IS
OR VEHICLE ON THE ROAD

UNIVERSAL SAFETY

Linda Dugeau *1940*

Born in 1913 and a graduate of Wellesley College, Linda Allen learned how to ride in 1932, when her boyfriend (and future husband) Bud Dugeau bought an old Harley-Davidson JD for fifteen dollars. Linda was a fast learner, and after only three lessons she caught the bug.

 After getting her own motorcycle in 1939, a 1937 Indian Junior Scout, Linda began to notice other women riders, mostly from pictures in motorcycle magazines. She started to correspond with several of these other lady riders; comparing notes, they discovered there were few activities for girl riders. Linda had heard about Amelia Earhart's club for women pilots, The Ninety-Nines, and decided it would be fun to form a similar group for women who rode motorcycles.

Linda wrote letters to dealers all over the country in search of interested women riders, a rarity back then. It took her and co-

founder Dot Robinson three years to find fifty-one women. In 1941 the Motor Maids of America officially received their A.M.A. Charter Number 509. Linda was the club's first secretary.

Linda fell in love with long distance touring. One summer she covered over 3,500 in two weeks, stopping long enough to visit the Harley-Davidson factory. Other trips took her up into remote parts of Canada.

In the early 1950s, Linda moved west to California, mainly so she could ride year round. Lucky to be able to combine her love for motorcycling with a paying job, for over twenty-five years Linda worked as a motorcycle courier in Los Angeles, delivering blueprints between construction jobs on her motorcycle. She often hosted off road tours in Southern California and even in the San Fernando Valley.

Linda was a true pioneer in the sport of motorcycling for women. She passed away on February 17, 2000 at the age of eighty-six.

1940
Linda on her Harley at a local motorcycle event around the time she was looking for other lady riders. Note name on the front fender.

Motor Maids

Circa 1939
Linda Dugeau, co-founder of the Motor Maids, on her 1937 Indian Junior Scout.
Motor Maids

Marge Hummel *1939*

Marjorie Dwyer grew up on a farm near Hurley, South Dakota where she became a rural schoolteacher. In 1935 she purchased a used 1935 Harley-Davidson motorcycle to commute to and from her farm and teaching job. In 1939 she bought herself a new 45 cubic-inch Harley-Davidson, which she nicknamed "Asthma" because of the way it coughed and spit.

When school closed for the summer, Marge took off for the summer with her nineteen-year-old sister Angie, also a teacher, as her passenger. The two adventurous girls rode the mostly gravel and unpaved roads on a long distance adventure that would take them to the Rocky Mountains and Pacific Northwest. They planned to spend their summer living on the road, taking along whatever would fit into one lone suitcase and their saddlebags.

After arriving in Tacoma, Washington the girls met up with two members of the Tacoma Club Motorcycle Club and decided to tag along as the rode to San Francisco to attend the 1939 World Exposition Fair. After enjoying the fair, the two girls headed back to South Dakota, stopping on the way to attend the 1939 Black Hills Motorcycle Classic.

At age twenty-five, Marge Dwyer had become the first female long distance rider to attend the famous Black Hills Rally. When they arrived home safe and sound, the total miles for their summer adventure was 6,070 miles.

Marge and Angie continued to ride together on several other long distance tours. In 1946, Marge married Lyle Hummel and they took over the Dwyer family farm where they settled down and raised their family.

Carl Edeburn

OPPOSITE: *Motorcyclist* **Magazine Cover** *1939*

For the June 1939 *Ladies Number* issue, *Motorcyclist* magazine used this cover with artwork depicting a futuristic woman rider. Her outfit is made of cellophane, which she wears over a bathing suit.

This entire issue was dedicated to the lady riders. Editor Chet Billings put out the request for stories and photos, and had such a huge response that they had to add four pages, more than any other issue in the history of the magazine.

Motorcyclist, *June 1939*

Motorcyclist

20c THE COPY
DOLLAR AND
A QUARTER
THE YEAR

Cellophane costume, over a bathing suit, and embodying boots, helmet and gauntlet gloves.

JUNE NINETEEN THIRTY-NINE

1940 to 1949

Do you have one in baby blue, to match my outfit?

OPPOSITE: 1940 Cartoon
"Do you have one in baby blue,
to match my outfit?"
Motorcyclist, *March 1940*

Mary Wall *Circa 1940*
Mary Wall of Fort Wayne, Indiana was an active member of the newly formed Atomic Riders Motorcycle
Club of Fort Wayne. A solo rider for over three years, Mary was also a member of the Motor Maids.

Motor Maids

Ruth "Sis" Baer Arnold *Circa 1940*

In the world that Ruth "Sis" Baer grew up in, it was all motorcycles, all the time—her first motorcycle trip was as a newborn, coming home from the hospital in a sidecar.

Her father, Frank "Fritzie" Baer, was a well known Indian dealer and factory representative in Springfield, Massachusetts who just happened to be one of the top hillclimbers in New England. He was a dominant force in motorcycling—his distinctive voice and extensive knowledge of the sport made him a respected official as well as a memorable announcer. Her brothers, Bobby and Butch were factory riders for Indian, while brother Tom worked the pits. Mother Louise Baer was an active member of the auxiliary to her father's riding club, "Fritzie's Roamers" where Sis was the auxiliary's club mascot. She learned to ride at an early age and developed life-long friendships with many of the predominant racers of the 1940s and 1950s, among them Ed Kretz and Dick Klamforth.

At age eighteen, her father Fritzie bought Sis her first motorcycle, a 1927 Prince. Later she owned an Indian State Police bike, which she taught her new husband Bob Arnold to ride. The bike was too hard for her to kickstart, so she traded it in for an Indian Warrior, and after that an Indian Arrow. When Sis married Bob Arnold in 1949 they both had motorcycles, but no car. When their first son Robert was born in 1951 Sis sold her motorcycle to pay the hospital bill. Later she wondered why they didn't keep her bike and sell Bob's!

They had two more boys, Tom born in 1953 and Peter in 1960, who both rode motorcycles early on.

Today, eighty year old Sis and husband Bob live in Florida and enjoy their grandchildren and great grandchildren. The pair will celebrate their sixtieth wedding anniversary in 2009.

Circa 1934
Sis Baer poses with famous Indian racer Ed Kretz.

Circa 1934
Thirteen-year-old Sis Baer in her Fritzie's Roamers mascot outfit at the National Championship Races in Laconia, New Hampshire.

Ruth and the Prince *1946*
Sis looks ready for Hollywood on her 1927 Indian Prince, a gift from her father.

Ruth at Laconia on her favorite bike, her 1949 Indian Arrow,
surrounded by the sons of Ralph Rogers, then president of Indian
Motorcycles.

All photos the Baer Family Library

Fourth of July Parade *1940*
Indian Motorcycles makes a statement for their 40th Anniversary at the Springfield, Massachusetts Fourth of July Parade.

Indian News, *August 1941*

Little idea I picked up at the dog races—keeps the boys happy

Both cartoons Motorcyclist, *January 1940*

June Lenz *1940*
June Lenz, daughter of famed hill climber Oscar Lenz, handled her Harley-Davidson like a veteran.

Motorcyclist, *August 1940*

I'm sorry John, but where I go my motorcycle goes

Doris Fisher *1940*
Doris Fisher, hailing from Westwood, New Jersey snapped on opening day at a popular fishing hole on the Pascac River.

Photo by W.T. Skinner, National Motorcycle Museum, Anamosa, Iowa

The light touch of a Woman's Hand!

Read what JULIA ADAMEC, *charming young motorcyclist, writes about the remarkable new* **MAGDRAULIC** *Electric Brake:*

"*During my seven motorcycle driving years this is indeed the finest feature I have had on any machine.*

I particularly admire the way the rear wheel holds the road when I apply my front wheel **MAGDRAULIC** *Electric Brake. Weighing 110 lbs., I need this smoother yet powerful stop to keep me in the saddle.*

In closing I do not hesitate in recommending **MAGDRAULIC** *Electric Brakes for all motorcycle drivers.*"

MAGDRAULIC ELECTRIC BRAKES
REG. U. S. PAT. OFF.

THE WORLD'S SAFEST BRAKE

CERTAIN IN EMERGENCIES . . . SMOOTHER IN TRAFFIC—The soft pressure of a woman's hand . . and the **MAGDRAULIC** front wheel Electric Brake brings JULIA ADAMEC's motorcycle to a smooth, even stop. Further movement of the hand controller, results in quicker, smoother stops at higher speeds.

SAVES MONEY—**MAGDRAULIC** hard molded linings, with their greater braking area, heat slowly, cool quickly. giving added life to the lining. No adjustments ever needed. Repair bills and tire purchases are fewer because reduced rear wheel braking cuts tire wear.

HOW IT WORKS—The attraction of the electro-magnet, energized by a current of very low amperage, to the armature disc which is turning with the wheel causes the lever to move in the direction of the wheel rotation. Frictional force on the end of the lever applies the brake shoes in proportion to the electro-magnetic force which is regulated by the hand pressure on the controller.

MANUFACTURERS: **MAGDRAULIC** Electric Brakes can be supplied to your specifications. Write for information.

DEALERS: Write for information concerning franchise rights.

EMPIRE ELECTRIC BRAKE CO.
NEWARK, NEW JERSEY

USE LESS CURRENT THAN YOUR TAIL LIGHT—

Enjoy a new sense of security . . . more comfort . . . safer driving with less rear wheel braking. Cut "rear wheel bounce" . . . end fatigue from "stop and go" traffic driving.

Front Wheel Brake Complete Including Wiring and Hand Controller

$22

F.O.B. Factory Ready for Installation

1. **COMFORT**—Smoother. No grab. No chatter.
2. **PLEASURE**—No tired leg muscles. Less fatigue.
3. **ECONOMY**—No adjustments. More tire mileage. Long lasting linings.
4. **EASE**—Finger-touch operation. Emergency stops with perfect control.
5. **SAFETY**—Stops in shorter distances. Stops in less time. Less "rear wheel bounce."
6. **EFFICIENCY**—Not affected by temperature of humidity. Premium performance from linings, even when hot from long hard use. Brakes will still operate even when battery is too low to start motor or light lights. "Ermalite" Brake Drum. Rigid cast backing plate.
7. **EASY TO INSTALL**—Takes less than one hour. No other parts or special tools required. No cutting No drilling. Instructions furnished.

GUARANTEED against defects for one year, or 10,000 miles

SAFER MOTOR CYCLING

SEND THIS COUPON FOR FREE BOOKLET "SAFER MOTORCYCLING"

EMPIRE ELECTRIC BRAKE CO. Newark, N. J.

Please send free booklet at no obligation.

NAME . . . .
ADDRESS . . . .
CITY & STATE . . . .
MAKE (*Model & Year*) . . . .
YOUR DEALER . . . .

PAT NO. 1,928,630
AND PATS. PENDING

ON HIGHWAY OR BYWAY

Go Firestone
—the Safe Way!

● Every road is a main road for the motorcyclist. His adventurous spirit takes him into the byways where new thrills and experiences await him, as well as onto the highways of the nation.

Wherever you ride—highway or byway—the safe way is the Firestone way. Equip your machine with Firestone Champion Motorcycle Tires—the year's outstanding contribution to motorcycling safety. Its patented Safety-Lock Gum-Dipped cord body provides maximum protection against blowouts and the deep, tough, rugged design of the Gear-Grip tread bites through road film and rain. Here's a tire that is safe on steepest layovers — one that gives you confidence wherever you ride.

Cruise this year with safety and economy. See your Firestone dealer today and have him equip your machine with a set of Firestone Champion Motorcycle Tires for greatest safety and longest mileage on the highway or the byway.

A TIRE FOR EVERY RIDING CONDITION!

THE NEW SPORTSMAN	THE NEW ALL NON-SKID	THE HIGH SPEED FOR ECONOMY
Combines long, rugged service with the ultimate in traction for all competitive events.	Designed with a heavier, tougher, deeper-cut tread for still greater safety and longer mileage. Ideal solo tire for rugged service.	This famous tire now available at a new low price. For high quality equip with Firestone High Speed Motorcycle Tires.

WATCH THE CHAMPIONS ★ THEY ALL RIDE ON FIRESTONE

1940
Firestone Tire Ad
"On Highway or Byway." Advertisement for Firestone tires.
Motorcyclist,
September 1940

Ruth Brenner *1940*

Ruth Brenner, lady Harley rider from Dayton, Ohio.

Motorcyclist, *June 1940*

Firestone Ad #2 *1940*

"Sweethearts on Parade. Hats off to the ladies, who enjoy this most thrilling of all sports."

Motorcyclist, *June 1940*

The San Francisco Motorettes *1940*

The San Francisco Motorettes were the first all-solo riders group for women riders. The main requirement for membership was that a girl had to ride solo. They held their own charter and were not an auxiliary of a men's club, which was often supposed.

Motorcyclist, *March 1940*

Girls IN THE SADDLE

YOU see them on every highway—alert, happy, carefree girls enjoying the great sport of motorcycling to the fullest. They handle their mounts with skill — they ride like veterans — they ride safely. They thrill to the joys of the open road and the healthful out-of-doors vitalizes their youth. Their chic riding togs and uniforms attract favorable attention everywhere. They lend distinction and class to our sport. Every day more and more girls take to motorcycling and become its enthusiastic followers. We welcome them and wish them glorious days in the saddle as they pilot their dependable mounts all over this great land of ours.

HARLEY-DAVIDSON MOTOR CO.
MILWAUKEE   •   WISCONSIN

1940 Harley-Davidson Ad
"Girls in the Saddle" advertisement for Harley-Davidson. Girl on left in large photo is Doris Fisher, from Westwood, New Jersey.
Harley-Davidson Archives, copyright H-D

Ruth Prindle *1940*

Ruth Prindle and her friend Connie Lambert took off from Niagara Falls on Ruth's '74 Harley-Davidson with plans to ride to Florida in 1940. With only a week's vacation and a bet from her friends that they couldn't make the 1,200 mile trip in two and a half days, Ruth was determined to meet her goal.

The pair enjoyed the scenery, riding through mountains of Pennsylvania and tobacco fields in Virginia and seeing sights they had never seen. The last day they encountered rain...for the entire day. Yet they still rode 520 miles, rain and all, reaching their goal— Niagara Falls to Florida—in two and a half days. They promptly sent a telegram to their friends to tell them they won the bet.

The tenacious duo rode through rain and hail and cold, but made it back safely. Their trip took them through nine states and the District of Columbia and covered 2,600 miles, all for very little expense.

Motorcyclist, *March 1940*

1940 Unknown Harley Rider

Her name might be unknown, but her spirit is clear for all to see.

OnlyClassics

Motorcyclist

20¢
THE COPY · DOLLAR
AND A QUARTER
THE YEAR

JUNE NINETEEN FORTY

*Motorcyclist
Ladies Issue*
Cover *1940*
Another artful
cover.
Motorcyclist,
June 1940

Mary Shephard Cutright *1940s*

Born in Chillicothe, Ohio, in 1918, Mary Shephard was always in love with two wheels. She raced bicycles at age fifteen, but longed for real speed. After high school, she got a job at a shoe factory with the goal of saving up enough money to buy herself a motorcycle. She got her first motorcycle at age nineteen, a 1937 45 cubic-inch Harley-Davidson.

Married to John Cutright in 1942 and a new mother in 1944, Mary kept right on riding. She even continued throughout the first seven months of her pregnancy. Baby Johnnie began riding on the front of mama's bike at the ripe old age of eight weeks, until he was old enough to sit on the back. Johnny traveled with his mother, and saw much of the country from the buddy seat.

Mary continued to ride though the war years. She rode her bike to her job at a Naval fireworks factory, though times were tough and there was a gas shortage. After the war, things were better and Mary rode as much as possible, mostly with male riders, but once in a while she would see another woman rider. Soon she learned about the Motor Maids and quickly became a member in 1949.

Mary loved her involvement with the Motor Maids, and in 1952 was appointed State Director of Southern Ohio. She worked hard and took on more positions within the club. At the 1966 Annual Motor Maids convention in Sturgis, South Dakota, Mary was elected President of the club, a position she held for twelve years.

Over her lifetime, Mary won numerous motorcycling awards and trophies, over 100 of them graced her home. Just over five feet tall, it took great skill to maneuver her big Harley Duo Glide in road runs and field meets, which included skill-testing events like pushing a barrel or riding on a thin plank.

Mary was a member of several other clubs, among them the A.M.A., the Chillicothe motorcycle Club and a charter member of the B.M.W. Owner's Club of Ohio.

Mary passed away on March 10, 1988 and was inducted into the National Motorcycle Hall of Fame in 1993 in the Leadership category, an honor for her incredible contributions to the sport she loved so much.

National Motorcycle Museum, Anamosa, Iowa

1941 Gabardine Breeches Ad

Advertisement for ladies gabardine riding breeches—for comfort and style.

Indian News, May 1941

Mercury Motorcycle Club *Circa 1940*

Woman modeling the official uniform shirt for the Mercury Motorcycle Club of Chicago.

Simmons Family Collection

TIPS TO PETTICOAT RIDERS

or
How to get a motorcycle in 10 Easy Lessons

by "Pat" Jennings

First: Get a license. This is an easy procedure with few drawbacks.

Second: Start borrowing the family car. Try to need it on the days father wants to attend his Boy Scout Leader meetings or when mother must go to the store.

Third: Get a job so you will have a little extra money; try to find one out of town where no one else goes at the time you must be at work, or where bus connections are poor.

Fourth: Win the family's confidence. Don't let bad weather conditions deter you from a 50 mile trip and start out in a huff, then turn around because you don't think it sensible.

Fifth: Go to bat for sister Sara and her house party imitations. She'll think motorcycles are great.

Sixth: Find an Indian dealer and get all the catalogues and price lists. Itemize all the advantages as:

1. Complete vision.
2. Central position of the rider for perfect control and judgment.
3. Advantage of outdoor activity and sport.
4. Economy-ideal for errands and for minimum expense when traveling.

Seventh: Present this to the family circle just after they have had their favorite dessert, but before they get buried in the evening paper. This is important. They must be in a receptive, broadminded mood so don't throw it at father before he dashes off to work. He'll have all day to think up answers and to listen to the boys diagram every flop they have seen since 1890.

Eighth: The family will suggest a second-hand car. Point out that you can't afford $15 a month for gas, oil, and repairs. Don't forget to remind them of the old Essex that was always falling apart.

Ninth: Take father over to the dealer's immediately just because you'd like to have him look things over. — Get the fellows to explain that it's "Show-off" Sammy who causes the accidents not the machine.

Tenth: Of course the dealer is on your side so work together. Have your deposit ready and the contract on the table. Give Dad the "old pal" pep talk and remind him of the days when you went fishing together.

The pen is ready and poised for the kill. "It's the Pioneers, Dad, who blaze the trail." Caramba! You made it! Your machine will be delivered as soon as possible. Congratulations.

Editor's Tip: Don't let the family see you reading this or they might be on guard.

Introducing **POWELL** *Aviate* 5-H.P.

5 Horse-Power
5 Speed Sensation

50 MILES PER HOUR
90 MILES PER GALLON

★ Heavy-Duty Built
★ Quick Pick-up
★ No Hill too Steep
★ Automatic Clutch
★ 3-1/16 Bore, 21 Cubic Inches
★ 16x4" Tires
★ Automobile Generator
★ Motorcycle Wet Battery
★ Engine Contains Parts from Popular Low-Priced Car

AUTO TOW EQUIPMENT

$159.50 PLUS TAX
F.O.B. Los Angeles

MODEL A-V-8

THE NEWEST SENSATION IN THE INDUSTRY!

Don't Delay — Investigate — Write Now to
Cooper Motors, Inc. 1101 SOUTH HOPE STREET LOS ANGELES, CALIFORNIA
POWELL MOTOR SCOOTER DISTRIBUTORS

Also 2½ Horsepower **POWELL** *Streamliner*

Dot Smith *1940*

San Francisco's Dorothy "Dot" Smith was a colorful member of the San Francisco Motorcycle Club—as were both her parents, Bertha and Bob Smith—which she joined as early as 1938, and the Motor Maids. She often won trophies as the "Best Dressed Lady Rider," yet she was also an extremely accomplished rider who could perform motorcycle stunts.

Dot Smith was also thought to be a member of the Bay City Motorcycle Club. Her bike is a 1939 61-cubic-inch Harley-Davidson EL Knucklehead which sold for $380.00 when new.

A.M.A. Archives

1940
Stunt rider Dot Smith. Was she really doing this?
Smith Family Collection

OVERLEAF: Riders in the News *1941*
"Fair Riders from Far Distant Points." A wonderful two-page spread.

Indian News

Dot Smith gets the long distance trophy for riding the farthest to the National Championship Rally.
Motorcyclist, July 1940

AMERICA'S PIONEER MOTORCYCLE

TRAIL BLAZERS

Indian

Indian Catalog Cover *1941* Colorful and picturesque, this catalog published by the Indian Motorcycle Company features a couple riding up in the hills. *Simmons Family Collection*

Mrs. Bill Anderson, wife of the well known competition rider of Houston, Texas.

FAIR RIDERS FROM

Miss Eleanore Sill on her 1941 Indian Sport Scout. Miss Sill has covered several thousand miles on her cycles in the past few years as a member of the Cleveland Indian Motorcycle Club.

Mrs. Helen Blansitt of St. Louis, Mo. on her Indian 4. This is Helen's second machine in her four years of solo riding and she reports the two children are as thrilled riding as she is.

Miss Betty Lou Mc-Farland of Clovis, New Mexico on her smooth handling Junior Scout.

Mrs. Jean Kulakowich of Yonkers, N. Y.

Miss Enes Pigozzo solo girl rider of West New York, New Jersey.

Lolly Greene of Wausau, Wisconsin on a recent trip to Rib Mountain. Lolly says, "Indian is the Aristocrate of Motorcycles."

R DISTANT POINTS

Mrs. Dot Kuntz, Indian booster from Dayton, Ohio. ▶

▼ Miss Wanda Stewart, popular girl rider and winner of the title "Miss Columbus, 1940", after a series of eliminations held in the theatres of Columbus, Ohio.

A neat rider on a new machine snapped in front of the A.M.A. booth at Laconia. ▶

Miss Polly Willingham of Spartanburg, South Carolina. ▶

▼ Flo Dietz, a member of the Cleveland Indians M/C with her sturdy Junior Scout about to take off for the Great Lakes M/C Time Run.

Mrs. Sarah Morgan, Birmingham, Alabama starting out for a ride. ▶

The Motor Maids *1941*

In the late 1930s a young enthusiast named Linda Dugeau of Providence, Rhode Island wanted to find other women who shared her love of motorcycles. Linda began writing letters to motorcycle dealers, riders and anyone she thought could help her locate these women. After a long search, she had a list of fifty-one riders, all of whom became the founding members of the Motor Maids. In 1941, they were issued Charter #509 of the American Motorcycle Association.

The goal of the Motor Maids has always been to unite women motorcyclists. Since formed, they still require members to own or operate their own motorcycle or one belonging to a family member.

Dot Robinson, of Detroit, Michigan became the first President. Dot held this position for twenty-five years until she resigned at the Motor Maids National Convention in 1965. Lou Riggsby was the first Vice-President, Linda Dugeau the first Secretary, Helen Kiss the first Treasurer and Hazel Duckworth the first Assistant Secretary.

The inaugural Motor Maids event was held in 1941 in Plainfield, New Jersey. The war effort and rationing made it hard to meet for the next two years, but in 1944 the Motor Maids met in Columbus Ohio for their first formal convention. Fifteen women from various states attended the meeting that Jane Farrow and Jo Folden co-hosted. From this meeting the club colors were decided upon: royal blue and silver-gray. Initially the uniforms were tailor-made of silver-gray gabardine with royal blue piping. It then evolved into gray slacks, a royal blue blouse with white tie, gloves and boots.

In 1941, Howard Foley, of Columbus, Ohio invited the Motor Maids to parade at the local Charity Newsies Race. They added white gloves to their uniform and thus they became known as the "Ladies of the White Gloves". Though they still ride in parades on occasion, the Motor Maids paraded annually at the Charity Newsies through their final year in 1979.

Each July, the Motor Maids hold a National Convention in a different part of the country. Interestingly enough they must ride to the convention, no trailers for these ladies! Once a member has attended two conventions and has ten consecutive active years of membership, she is eligible for Life Membership. Silver Life Membership requires twenty-five years of active membership and attendance at five conventions. When a member attends ten conventions during her fifty years of active membership she is awarded the Motor Maids prestigious Golden Life Membership.

Since the beginning and throughout the years of their existence the Motor Maids have been held in high esteem. Their founding sisters would be proud of what they help to create over six decades ago.

Circa 1940s
Motor Maids at lunch. Dot Robinson sips her coffee.
Graphic Photos, Des Moines, Iowa

1947
Motor Maid
Convention,
Singing Pines,
Nashville,
Indiana, July
13, 1947.
Motor Maids

Circa 1947
Motor Maids

1949
Motor Maids

1949

Motor Maids, Ohio Caverns Tour. Eighteen Motor Maids and their guests took part in a meeting in Bellefontaine, Ohio on April 30–May 1, 1949. Some of the activities planned for the weekend were a trip through historic Piatt Castle and a tour to the famous Ohio Caverns; a banquet and a parade that circled through the main section of town.

Girls attending were (first row, from left), Evelyn Dane; Pearl Louise Smith; Motor Maid President Dot Robinson; Mabel Aston; Mary Wall; Mary Williams; Jane Penrod; (second row, from left) Vice President Evelyn Bawden; Secretray Vera Griffin; Helen Vaughan; Bernice Miles; Grace Hall; Helen Smith; (third row, from left) Martha Smith; a guest, Ann Sargent; a guest, Norma Doner; Donna Lou Miller; and Gwen Tedjeske.

Motor Maids

1950
Motor Maids at Pekin. Attending the Motor Maids two day rally in Pekin, Illinois on September 23 and 24, 1950 were: (from left front row) Lucille Moody, Elizabeth Tassart, Anna Lehr Boon, Heida Cowan, Agnes Potter, Florence Cook, Rosella Graff; (from left, back row) Helen Vaughn, Ilene Clausen, Helen Blansitt, Alena Strasser, Bernice Miles, Dorothy Mercer, Louise Stokes, Virginia Simms and Caroline Bell.

Motor Maids

1950
Motor Maids. Taken at the Cumberland, Maryland Meet on May 7, 1950. Marge Cosgrove, Helen Paul and Kate Miller.

Motor Maids

Jean Kulakowich *Circa 1941*
Jean Kulakowich from Yonkers, New York in front of Little Bob's Indian Sales.

Esta Manthos Indian Motorcycle Collection, Museum of Springfield History, Springfield, Massachusetts

1941 Servi-Cycle Ad
Advertisement for the Simplex Servi-Cycle, another economical means of transportation from the Simplex Manufacturing Company of New Orleans.

Motorcyclist, August 1940

Gloria Tramontin Struck *1941*

Gloria's first bike was an Indian Pony at age sixteen, but her motorcycling days really started long before that. She was born in 1925 in an apartment attached to her family's motorcycle shop in Clifton, New Jersey. The Lexington Motorcycle Shop was started in 1915 and sold all brands of motorcycles before it eventually evolved into Tramontin Harley-Davidson some years later. When her father died in 1928, Gloria's mother continued to run the shop. Her older brother Arthur, or "Bub", taught her how to ride when she was sixteen even though she didn't really want to. Bub was a professional hillclimber right up until he retired at age seventy-eight even though he is still riding at age eighty-nine.

Gloria's second bike was a used 1941 Indian Bonneville Scout which she rode during the war years. After the war, she bought a brand new 1946 Indian Chief. In 1950 she started riding Harleys and has had ten of them since. (She currently rides a 2004 Harley-Davidson Heritage Softail Classic.)

To get her motorcycle operator's license, Gloria rode forty-five miles to Hackettstown, New Jersey for the test. It was a long ride back then, over a lonely two lane road. When she got to the testing area, the instructor waved her over and asked, "Where are you from?" "Clifton, New Jersey", she replied. "How did you get your motorcycle here?" he asked, looking around to see if there was a man with her. "I rode it", she replied quietly. "Well, you don't need to take a test here, if you rode that thing all the way from Clifton, I guess you know how to ride."

In 1946 Gloria joined the Motor Maids and has been a member for sixty-three years—making her a Golden Life Member. She has ridden her bike to every state on the continent, and some states many times over.

Gloria is a rider's rider! In 1950 she took off on her first solo long distance trip to Canada from her home in New Jersey, stopping to visit another Motor Maid, Marilyn Oler, who lived in Ohio. Marilyn decided to go with her and the two of them rode to Toronto and Montreal, stopping along the way to take in the sights. Their adventure was featured in the December 1952 issue of Harley-Davidson's *Enthusiast* magazine.

Gloria and her son Glenn, also a rider, have ridden all over Europe. In 1999 they tackled many mountain passes: one of the most challenging of all was the Passo dello Stelvio in the Italian Alps with eighty-two hairpin turns. On their second trip in 2001 they rode more than 4,000 miles in eight countries.

Not one to ever put her bike on a trailer, in 2003, at age seventy-eight, Gloria rode the 7,450 mile roundtrip to the Motor Maids Convention in Chico, California from New Jersey and in 2007 Gloria rode 6,000 roundtrip to the M.M. convention in Post Falls, Idaho.

Gloria does not seem to let anything slow her down. On March 1, 2008 Gloria and her daughter, Motor Maid Lori DeSilva, took off on their bikes for an over 1,000 mile journey to Daytona Beach, Florida for the yearly gathering at Bike Week.

She is looking forward to riding many more miles in years ahead, including plans for a cross-country motorcycle trip at age ninety. Her motto is: "Have dreams and live them!"

1925

Gloria's parents are pictured in front of their motorcycle shop in this 1925 photograph. Her dad is leaning on the gas pump standing next to Gloria's mother, who was pregnant with Gloria at the time. Her older brother, Bud, wearing his cowboy outfit is in the foreground. Dog Jimmy is howling in the sidecar.

1950

Gloria and her Harley-Davidson on her first long distance trip from New Jersey to Canada.

All photos, Gloria Tramontin Struck

1942 Clinton, Iowa
Unknown rider on
her 1937 Indian Chief.
Taken on July 4, 1942,
in Clinton, Iowa.
*National Motorcycle
Museum, Anamosa, Iowa*

Agnes *Sunny* Sonnenfelt *1943*

While other girls of her age were playing with dolls, Agnes *Sunny* Sonnenfelt was tinkering with her brother's bug roadster, tearing it apart and putting it back together. In high school, she had her own motorcycle she called *Josephine.*

W.A.A.C. Auxiliary, Agnes 'Sunny' Sonnenfelt, of Eau Claire, Wisconsin was Camp Abbott's first female motorcyclist. When Sonnenfelt reported to Sergeant Anthony for duty as a dispatch rider, he was frankly skeptical. He went to great pains to explain the operation of a cycle to the new auxiliary and then told her to hop aboard and take a turn around the area, but cautioned *take it easy.* Sonnenfelt demonstrated her skill—and made the machine do everything but talk.

Sunny was recognized as an accomplished motorcyclist and traveled throughout the United States on her machine.

Sunny toured the west coast in 1941 on a solo tour in which she covered 7,500 miles. Previous to joining the W.A.A.C.s she was Midwestern director of the Motor Maids of America. She rode daily from post headquarters, Camp Abbott, to Bend, Oregon, the nearest town to post, eighteen miles, carrying military dispatches.

Indian News, *June/July 1943, cover*

Vera Griffin *1942*

Born in 1914 Vera Griffin, of
Greensburg, Indiana was a
rider's rider, logging over a
million miles in over sixty
years of riding through the
lower forty-eight states, Mexico
and Canada.

Along with her husband
Johnnie, Vera founded the
Stoney Lonesome Motorcycle
Club in 1940. By 1942 Vera
was already on her fourth
motorcycle.

Also an accomplished long
distance rider, Vera completed
an incredible 10,000 mile
ride in 1948. She also rode a
grueling 1,000 miles in a twenty-
four hours endurance ride, and
competed in many other "All
Girl" events over the years. In
field events, and scored well
against the men. She was a
founding member of the Motor
Maids, and even worked as a
welder for a time.

Vera passed away age the
age of eighty-one in 1994.
A Harley girl to the end, Vera's
casket was lovingly draped with
an orange and black Harley-
Davidson flag.

Shown here, Vera poses on
her third Harley-Davidson, a gift
from her husband Johnnie.

Vera Griffin Collection
and the Motor Maids

Pat Boatright *Circa 1945*
Pat Boatright started riding in 1938 and was very active in the Motor Maids, acting as the Texas State
Director of the Motor Maids in the late 1940s.

Motor Maids

Betty Jeremey *1946*

A Charter member of the Motor Maids, Betty Jeremey of Lake George, New York owned and rode her own Indian Sport Scout. Here she is pictured at Laconia, New Hampshire in 1946.

National Motorcycle Museum, Anamosa, Iowa

Indian Riders at Caledonia

1946

Riders lined up at the Caledonia Fairgrounds, near Rochester, New York. The only known rider is on the white Indian, Louise Scherbyn.

Frank Zimmy *Zimmerman Collection, Rochester, New York*

1946 Mabel Aston

Motor Maid Mabel Aston, of Parkersburg, West Virginia. Photo taken at Lockport, Ohio 1946.

Simmons Family Collection

Slow Race Winners
Circa 1946
Winners of the Girl's Slow Race.
Left to right, Jackie Varney, Mrs.
Rene King, Edi Lynn, and two
unknown riders.

Norman Speirs Photography

Theresa Karpowich and Ralph Rogers *1946*
Sitting on a new Indian Chief,
Indian rider Theresa Karpowich
talks with President of the
Indian Motorcycle Company
Ralph Rogers at Laconia, New
Hampshire in 1946. Rogers was
the President of Indian from
1945 to 1949.

*Esta Manthos Indian Motorcycle
Collection, Museum of Springfield
History, Springfield, Massachusetts*

All Girl Motorcycle Show Poster
1947
Poster advertisement from the All Girls Motorcycle Show, Waterloo, New York.
Simmons Family Collection

ALL GIRLS
MOTORCYCLE
SHOW!
(FIELD MEET)
A. M. A. SANCT. 10927

Fair Grounds, Waterloo, N. Y.

Sunday, August 17, 1947
At 2:30 P. M., D. S. T.

SEE AMERICA'S ALL GIRL RIDERS IN ACTION

FREE GRANDSTAND

Admission · 60c Tax Inc.

WA-CO-MO Pals Motorcycle Club
NEWARK, N. Y.

1947 Dixie
A gal named Dixie rides into Marin County, California in 1947.

Ernie Magri Collection

Edna Renfrow
1947
Motor Maid Edna Renfrow, Fort Wayne, Indiana, 1947.

Simmons Family Collection

Vickie Hughes *1947*
In 1947 Vickie Hughes was the only woman in the Tamalpais Motorcycle Club of San Anselmo, California who actually rode her own bike!

Ruth Smith on a Triumph *1947*

Vickie Hughes makes it look easy as she pilots her Indian through a muddy patch along the back roads of Marin County, California, 1947.

Vickie "Pickles" Hughes, left, and George Smith, navigate the rolling hills of Marin County, California, just north of San Francisco, 1947.

In 1947 Satch Parez, left, and Vickie Hughes, were members of the Tamalpais Motorcycle Club in San Anselmo, California. "Vickie sure could ride the big V-twins, no question about it," recalled club founder Ernie Magri.

Vickie Hughes on an Indian, left, and friend Ruth Smith on a Triumph, at the B Street Bar in San Anselmo, California, 1947.

All photos, Magri Family Collection

American Motorcycling

THE GREATEST SPORT IN THE WORLD

Vol. II No. 7   JULY 1948 $2 Year 20¢ Copy

NORTHERN PEACHES AND A GEORGIA BROADSLIDER

American Motorcycling **Cover**

July, 1948 cover of *American Motorcycling* magazine featuring members of the Motor Maids. From left to right, Betty Robinson Fauls, Dot Robinson, unknown, Linda Dugeau, unknown, unknown and Vera Griffin.

  The little boy on the small sized Indian motorcycle is Teddy Edwards, son of Ted Edwards, the National T.T. 50 Mile Champion Racer. Teddy, known as the *Blonde Bomber*, started riding at age three.

American Motorcycling, *July 1948*

"Start of a Long Friendship!"
1948 Baldwin-Duckworth Ad
American Motorcyclist, *August 1948*

Grace Flynn *1948*
Miss Grace Flynn models the new 1948 Indian Roadmaster, one of three new models Indian offered for the year.

Esta Manthos Indian Motorcycle Collection, Museum of Springfield History, Springfield, Massachusetts

Start of a Long Friendship!

There are years of cycling pleasure ahead—tens of thousands of miles of exciting travel. The smooth, dependable performance built into to-day's new motorcycles assures it!

Playing an important part in this friendship is Duckworth Roller Chain. Smoothly and lastingly this leading cycle chain transmits the surging power from motor to wheel. It's the dependable, economical, positive drive that's backed by thousands of owners and millions of miles of operation.

Roll on Duckworth Roller—
the cycle-right chain!

Sold by Dealers Everywhere

BALDWIN - DUCKWORTH
Baldwin-Duckworth - Division of Chain Belt Company
381 Plainfield Street, Springfield 2, Massachusetts

Jane Russell *1948*

Famous actress and "sweater girl" Jane Russell was actually a motorcycle fan. Crazy about motorcycles her whole life, Jane used to ride as a passenger with her brothers, who were enthusiastic riders. After marrying Los Angeles Rams football star Bob Waterfield, Jane would often mention to him that she wanted her own motorcycle someday. At first he protested—he didn't know anyone whose wife rode a motorcycle—and it didn't seem very *ladylike*.

Apparently, Jane's close friend Jeannie (whom Bob greatly admired) happened to own a motorcycle. Jeannie explained to him that she had learned about motorcycles from her husband and riding was something she really loved. Bob was sold and soon he and Jane bought the two Indians.

Jane, being into fashion and designing some of her own clothing, often thought about designing some riding outfits for herself and other women riders.

Photo by Raphael G. Wolff, Hollywood, California
Esta Manthos Indian Motorcycle Collection, Museum of Springfield History, Springfield, Massachusetts

Lizabeth Scott in the *Indian News* *Circa 1948*
Pictured riding a 1948 Indian Scout on the R.K.O. Pictures Lot is actress Lizabeth Scott, who appeared in twenty-one films between 1945 and 1957.

To launch their new 1948 models, Indian hired a New York ad agency who began a publicity campaign that featured actresses, models and sport stars to help gain attention and enhance the image of Indian motorcycles.

Esta Manthos Indian Motorcycle Collection, Museum of Springfield History, Springfield, Massachusetts

Mothers and Daughters
1948
Female motorcycle club members and their children pose with a 1948 Harley-Davidson FL.

Harley-Davidson Archives, copyright H-D

Indian Arrow Postcard
1949
Advertisement for the new Indian Arrow.

Simmons Family Collection

Ruth Steiner and Friend *1949*
Photo of Motor Maids Ruth Steiner and friend, taken fall of 1949 showing the latest Harley-Davidson motorcycles. Gormans' Harley-Davidson was later Wallace Harley-Davidson and then Shreveport Harley-Davidson.

Sandy Steiner, son of Ruth Stein, Chrome Fusions, Inc.

Rudy Gee *1949*
The first time Rudy Gee entered a Class B sidecar run in Columbus, Ohio, she rode to victory with a score of 998 points. She competed against the men, with her husband, Joe, a long time enduro rider, along as her passenger.

Rudy Gee started riding in 1936, her usual mount being a 1936 Indian Scout. The motorcycle she piloted in the run was an Indian '45 with an interesting left-hand sidecar.

Simmons Family Collection

Lu Magri and Her Scat *1949*
Lu Magri of Rio Linda, California's first bike was a 1942 Harley-Davidson 45 cubic-inch refurbished from military surplus. "It had a purple and grey metal-flake paint job and a bobbed rear fender" said Lu. "My daughter Terrie wouldn't let me leave for work on it without giving her a ride first".

Shown here in 1949 is Lu aboard her 165cc Harley-Davidson Scat. Lu and her husband Armando, a former racer, bought the Harley-Davidson dealership in Sacramento, California in 1950.

Magri Family Collection

Cookie Ayers Crum *1949*

While she was supposed to be learning shorthand, fifteen-year-old Cookie heard and saw every motorcycle that passed by her window at Sarasota High School. She wasn't into boys or school, her love was motorcycles and someday she knew she would ride one!

Someday came in 1946 when a boy named Kenny Kennedy taught Cookie to ride when she was sixteen years old. He would pick her up in his car, she would throw her boots out the bedroom window, pick them up and off they would go in his car to get his 1937 Harley-Davidson '74.

On a family trip to Chicago's Riverview Park, Cookie saw her first motor drome wall of death show. She was hooked as she watched over and over again as the riders raced up and down the wall. Little did she know what was in store.

In 1949, when Cookie was nineteen, she spotted an ad for "The World of Mirth Show" in the *Sarasota Herald* that read, "Travel and Adventure, will teach personable girl with nerve and courage to become a motorcycle exhibition rider in a Motor Drome". She applied and was chosen for the job, soon to be billed as "Cookie Ayers (Ayers was a show name), Queen of the Daredevils". The only problem was that Cookie needed to learn to ride the 1929 Indian Scout on the wall. It took about a month of practice for her to master it.

During the next several years Cookie married and gave birth to her daughter (Michele), and divorced. She raised Michele by herself along with help from her fellow "carnies" as they traveled the country with the Motor Drome show. She lived with Michele in the back of the semi-trailer that held the walls she rode on. Cookie continued to ride the wall for eight years, summers up north at the fairs and winters in Florida at some of the "still" dates.

Motorcycles and motorcycling remained a constant in Cookies life after she left the wall. She was Motor Maid for many years and became a Harley-Davidson dealer in Portland, Oregon. In 1985, Cookie married a wonderful guy named Bob Crum, and thus became Cookie Crum!

Today, Cookie is happily retired and still lives in Portland, Oregon.

Cookie is to be inducted into the Sturgis Motorcycle Hall of Fame in August 2009.

1949 World of Mirth show: Russ Pelaquin, Cookie and Billy McCombs on the Bally.

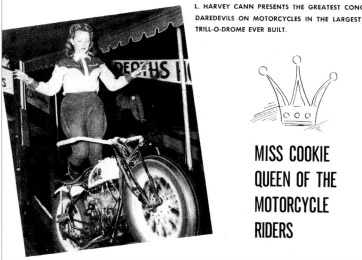

L. HARVEY CANN PRESENTS THE GREATEST CONGRESS OF DAREDEVILS ON MOTORCYCLES IN THE LARGEST TRILL-O-DROME EVER BUILT.

MISS COOKIE QUEEN OF THE MOTORCYCLE RIDERS

1949 A page from World of Mirth program.

1949
View of wall of death from the outside.

Circa 1950
World of Mirth show, waiting for the crowd.

All photos Cookie Crum

Circa 1950
Cookie riding no-hands on the wall.

1950

AMERICAN Motorcycling

VOL. IV No. 5 $2 YEAR 25c COPY   MAY, 1950

The Greatest Sport in the World

Bettie Binkley
1950
Cover Girl Betty
Binkley of Nashville,
Tennessee fixes
her hair in the rear
view mirror.
     American
     Motorcycling,
     May 1950

OPPOSITE:
The Tin Toy
Motorcycle Girls
Circa 1950
Made in Japan by
HAJI.
     Photo by Patrick
     Simmons, Simmons
     Family Collection

Margaret Wilson *1950*

Originally from Wisconsin, Margaret Wilson's love affair with motorcycling started in 1946 when her husband, Mike, bought her a 1946 45-cubic-inch Harley-Davidson. The bike was so high off the ground, Margaret's feet dangled—so Mike would ride behind her on the bike and put his feet down when they stopped. Soon after Margaret took off on her own—and never looked back, putting on over 550,000 miles all over the U.S. and Canada. In one year alone, Margaret traveled to all forty-eight contiguous states and nine Canadian Provinces.

For twenty-five years, Margaret and Mike ran Wilson's Motorcycle Sales in Cedar Rapids, Iowa. Through those years and beyond, Margaret has been a tremendous motorcycle supporter. She has been a Motor Maid since 1951, and helped form the Corn State Riders Motorcycle Club in the early 1950s, acting as secretary and road captain. She was also the only woman rider on the club's motorcycle drill team.

In 2003 Margaret was awarded the A.M.A. Bessie Stringfield Award, a distinguished honor awarded to women who are leaders in motorcycling.

In 2004 she was inducted into both the National Motorcycle Hall of Fame and the American Motorcycle Association Hall of Fame. She is also proud to be a Golden Life Member of the Motor Maids.

Margaret Wilson at the Harley-Davidson Factory *1951*

Margaret told me that this photograph was taken in the fall of 1951 Here she is sitting on a Harley-Davidson K Model. The story is that she and husband Mike (they were Harley dealers at the time), were riding to an open house at the Harley factory in Milwaukee for a preview of new models not yet available to the public. A man rode up next to her on a new looking motorcycle and noticed she was looking intently to see what it was, since it was a totally new machine. They stopped down the road and he asked her if she would like to test ride it and switch bikes. She did, and became one of the first of the public to ride the new 1952 K Model, picured here.

Wheels Through Time Motorcycle Museum

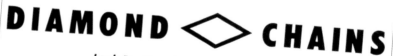
Diamond Chain Ad *1950*

American Motorcycling, *November 1950*

Ilene Clausen
1950
Motor Maid Ilene
Clausen from
Chicago, Illinois.
*Photo by Van Westrop
Studio, Illinois, National
Motorcycle Museum,
Anamosa, Iowa*

WHEN IN BOSTON
VISIT OUR STORES

Featuring
INDIAN
A. J. S.
MATCHLESS
NORTON
VINCENT
CHEK
JAWA
Motorcycles

- FINEST NEW ENGLAND MOTORCYCLE HOSPITALITY
- PARTS AND SERVICE FOR ALL MAKES
- EVERY KNOWN ACCESSORY ON DISPLAY

THREE STORES IN BOSTON AREA

Andrews Indian Motorcycle Sales
81 W. Concord St. Tel. CIrcle 7-9677 Boston

Chaisson Indian Sales
15 Spring St. Tel. WA 4-9340
WATERTOWN

Spinzola Indian Sales
Rockland St., West End Tel. 6-2130
HINGHAM

Indian Motorcycle Ad *1950*

Indian advertisement for East Coast publication.

Motorcycling Digest, *1950*

A Little Heart-Warmer

Now she can have a jacket just like yours. Buco makes this lady's version of their man's motorcycle jacket. Tailored from tanned horsehide, it is fashioned to drape gracefully to the figure. It is full-cut, has a free-action, self-folding back, and a black rayon quilted lining—100 per cent wool insulated. She'll be as warm as a hot toddy on a frosty morn, and the thanks you'll get when she finds this under her tree will be twice as fervent. Then, of course, there are the two zipper pockets (with a patch pocket effect) and the good looking belt. Your dealer sells these "warm friendship" items for a cool $29.50. They're made by the Joseph Buegeleisen Company.

Buco Jacket Ad *1950*

Who says there were no leather riding jackets made for women back in 1950? This "Little Heart Warmer" fit the bill and looks as though it fit like a glove.

American Motorcycling, *November 1950*

Mary McCanna *1950*

Harley-Davidson rider, Mary McCanna parks her Harley. She's wearing the popular Harley hat of the era.

American Motorcycling, *November 1950*

Irene Teeter
Circa 1950
Motor Maid
Irene Teeter
from Rochester,
New York
wearing her
Motor Maids
uniform. She
tops it off
with a classic
motorcycle
hat adorned
with pin and
patches.
Motor Maids

Mary Jane Loberg *1950*

Jane grew around motorcycles for much of her young life near Minneapolis. Her father was into motorcycles, and as a small girl Jane would often help him in his workshop. Her boyfriend Norman (and later husband) had a Henderson, and he taught Jane to ride. They married when Jane was 18, and sold the Henderson soon after.

After their honeymoon they settled into married life and began to miss their motorcycle. Norman bought an Army surplus military Harley-Davidson 45 that needed some work, and eventually the couple were back on the road.

A year or so later, Norman picked up a basket-case Harley 45 and got it running for Jane to ride. He soon worked on making the bike fit Jane's tiny four-foot eleven-inch frame. The bike was equipped with an adapter kit that used a foot shifter and a hand clutch. The bike was also lowered and Norman made a special lowered seat. He also created a set of thick wooden soles for Jane's riding boots.

The couple joined the Gopher State Motorcycle Club and began to participate in many of the touring and field events.

Jane made her first visit to Sturgis with Norman on this bike in 1948. They camped in City Park in their two-man pup tent.

While in Sturgis, her husband would often "hang out with the boys." Jane sought out the company of some of the other women and learned about the Motor Maids, which she eventually joined.

Jane became friends with two other Motor Maids from Minneapolis, Kathy Anderson and Dot Fiscette. All three women were active in the Bloomington Elementary School PTA. In those days it was not all that acceptable to be a woman rider. "We were careful to never let any of the other PTA mother's know about our passion," Jane said. On sunny afternoons, when all of their children were in school, the three women would go for afternoon rides. One of the neighbors, after seeing two helmeted riders (Kathy and Dot) show up at her house and then watch Jane ride off with them down the street, started a rumor that Jane was running off with two male motorcyclists every other afternoon.

At 88 years of age, Mary Jane Loberg lives with her grandson in Bloomington, Minnesota.

Carl Edeburn

AMERICAN Motorcycling

VOL. IV No. 11 $2 YEAR 25¢ COPY   NOVEMBER, 1950

RIDING THE PLANK (Page 7)

The Greatest Sport in the World

Iva Dean Griffin

1950

Gracing the cover of the *American Motorcycling* is fifteen-year-old Iva Dean Griffin from Cleveland, Tennessee. With a determined look on her face, Iva rides the plank at the 1950 Atlanta, Georgia Gypsy Tour.

Photo by Paul Robertson, American Motorcycling

Index

Ace motorcycle, 111
A. D. Farrow Co., 126–129
Adams, Kathryn, 117
Adamec, Julie, 198
Alexander, Mrs. H. G., 90
Althoff, Bob and Valerie, 128
Altop, Mrs. Herman, 52
Anderson, Kathy, 238
Anderson, Mrs. Bill, 208
Apple, Mickey, 137
Arnold, Ruth Baer, 194–195
Aston, Mabel, 212, 220
Atomic Riders Motorcycle Club, 193

Baker, Gyp, 15, 178
Bales, Vivian, 154
Barley, Mrs. A. L., 69
Bawden, Evelyn, 212
Bay City Motorcycle Club, 206
Bell, Caroline, 213
Bennett, Mrs. Wells, 147
Berg, Miss, 95
Berkley, Edna, 126
Bethel, Hazel, 170–171
Bice, Mrs. John E., 122
Bilty, Hazel, 1, 117
Binkley, Bettie, 233
Bixby, Mrs., 60
Blansitt, Helen, 208, 213
Boatright, Pat, 218
Boon, Anna Lehr, 213
Borek, Muriel, 146
Brady, Alice, 133
Brenner, Ruth, 200
Briggs & Stratton motor scooter, 114
Britton, Sterling, 103
Bromwell, Laura, 127
Brown, Will, 18
Brucess, Bessie, 55
Buchanan, Mrs. Crede, 172
Buckeye Motorcycle Club, 128, 185
Burnham, Florence, 174

C'Dora, 29
Chaplin, Charlie, 120
Chapple, A. G., 37
Chicago Motorcycle Club, 40, 141
Christiansen, Mrs. M., 96
Clark, Ann, 171
Clark, Mrs. C. B., 26, 141
Clausen, Ilene, 213, 235
Clements, Mrs. Charles, 158
Cleveland motorcycle, 90, 92, 95, 101, 114, 138
Clifford, Mrs. George W., 170
Clymer, Mrs. Floyd, 122, 139
Conklin, Edna, 106
Cook, Florence, 213
Corn State Riders Motorcycle Club, 234
Cosgrove, Marge, 213
Cowan, Heida, 213
Crewe, Della, 62
Crosse, Esther A., 99
Crum, Cookie Ayers, 230–231
Culip, Viola, 14
Cummings, Jennie, 127
Currid, Evelyn, 160, 162–163
Curtiss, 34
Cutright, Mary Shephard, 204

Dane, Evelyn, 212

Davidson, Karen, 6–7
Davidson, Mrs. Seth, 147
Delage, Frances, 106
DeSilva, 215
Detroit Motorcycle Club, 28
Dettmer, Lucy Jacke, 22
Dietz, Flo, 209
Doerman, Al & Pat, 128
Doll, Mrs. Carl, 144
Doner, Norma, 212
Doyle, Catherine, 111
Dreher, Mrs. W. R., 51
Duck, 34
Duckworth, Hazel, 211
Dugeau, Linda, 15, 188–189, 210, 225

Earhart, Amelia, (Ninety-Nines, The) 86, 188
Emblem, 51
Emde, Florence, 177
Erol, Jane, 105
Evans Power Cycle, 122, 141
Excelsior, 44, 58–59, 63, 77–78, 88–89, 91, 95, 97, 159

Farrow
    Dorothy, 128, 132
    Jane, 130, 210
    Lillian, 128–129
Fauls, Betty Robinson, 225
Federation of American Motorcyclists (F.A.M.), 22, 51
Feilbach Limited, 46–47
Fiscette, Dot, 238
Fisher, Doris, 197, 201
Flanders motorcycle, 4, 35
Flynn, Grace, 226
Flynn, Margaret, 143
Folden, Jo, 210
Forbes-Johnson, Polly, 176
Free, Mrs. Roland, 158
Fritzie's Roamers, 194

Gallan, Mavis, 165
Gast, Margaret, 18–21
Gee, Rudy, 229
Gill, Nellie Joe, 130–131
Gold, Bobby, 132
Gopher State Motorcycle Club, 238
Goudy, Agnes, 97
Goulding sidecars, 148
Graff, Rosella, 213
Gray, Doris, 125
Greene, Lolly, 208
Greenwald, Freda, 127
Griffin, Iva Dean, 239
Griffin, Vera, 15, 212, 217, 225
Groat, Pauline, 166

Hack, Anna T., 60
Hager, Olive, 15, 134–136
Halden, Marge, 178
Hall, Grace, 212
Hall, Ruth, 160, 162–163
Harley-Davidson, 8, 32, 34, 36, 43, 62, 74, 83, 93, 95, 98, 102, 106, 113, 116–117, 128, 131, 133, 148, 154–155, 161, 172, 174, 188, 196, 201–202, 204, 206, 215, 229, 234
Hauerwas, Lillian, 49, 93
Haughey, Mrs. James, 69
Heaps, Lillian Slaughter, 42

Henderson motorcycle, 50, 66, 238
Henry, Constance, 50
Herbert, Dotty, 174
Hildabrand, Fay & Mrs. J. S., 74
Hodges, Mrs., 60
Hogg, Mrs. John E., 102
Hollander, Bessie, 126
Holmes, Helen, 116
Hopper, Ruth, 54
Hotchkiss, Effie & Avis, 14, 64–65
Hughes, Vickie, 224
Hummel, Angie, 190
Hummel, Marge, 190

Indian, 14, 42, 50, 59, 67, 69, 78–79, 81, 86, 92, 99, 110, 116, 118, 120, 139, 140, 143–146, 152, 155, 158, 166–168, 171–172, 174, 184, 186–189, 194–196, 207–209, 214–216, 219, 221, 224, 228–229, 236
Indian-Cygnet, 96
Inge, Clara, 32
Irons, Maude, 100

Jeremey, Betty, 219
Johnson, Margaret, 166
Johnson Motor Wheels, 109, 119

Karpowich, Theresa, 221
Karslake, Alice, 34
Karslake, Margaret, 36
Kelly, Katherine, 38–39
Kemp, Marjorie, 15, 159
Kern, Maude, 59
King, Rene, 221
Kiss, Helen, 164–165, 210
Kretz, Ed, 194
Kulakowich, Jean, 208, 214
Kuntz, Dot, 209

LaFrance, Lillian, 142
Lake, Mabel, 160, 162–163
Lambert, Connie, 202
Lang, Mrs. John, 95
Langley, Jane Farrow, 130
Latterman, Mrs. E. T., 101
Lester, Grace, 42
Legion of Mad Speed Demons, 159
Lenz, Julie, 196
Lenz, Mrs. Oscar, 123
Loberg, Mary Jane, 238
Loeb, Frances L., 78
Los Angeles Motorcycle Club, 48
Lynn, Edi, 221

Maddi, Josephine, 162–163
Magnet Lightweights, 27
Magri, Lu, 229
Marsh & Metz Effie, 62
Mason, Mrs. Harry G., 95
Masters, Mabel, 14
Matthews, Vera, 46
McCanna, Mary, 236
McCord, Ruth, 78, 81
McFarland, Betty Lou, 208
Meisel, Dorothy, 160, 162–163
Mercer, Dorothy, 213
Mercury Motorcycle Club, 204
Merkel motorcycles, 18–19, 21, 31, 34, 38–39
Miles, Bernice, 212–213
Miller, Donna Lou, 212
Miller, Kate, 213
Milwaukee Motorcycle Club, 93

Moody, Lucille, 213
Morgan, Sarah, 209
Motor Maids, 15, 130–131, 148, 151, 164, 166, 184, 188–189, 194, 204, 206, 210–220, 223, 225, 229, 234–235, 237–238

Nelson, Vivian, 180
Ner-A-Car, 123, 141

Nichols, Anna, 145
Ninety-Nines, The (see Earhart, Amelia)
Normand, Mabel, 120

Oler, Marilyn, 215
Orange County Motorcycle Club, 161

Paige, Barney, 125
Pakonian, Emma Louise (see Apple, Mickey)
Parritt, Emma, 99
Parrott, Velma, 145
Paul, Helen, 213
Pelaquin, Viola, 153
Penrod, Jane, 212
Peterson, Fannie, 145
Pigozzo, Enes, 208
Pope, 70–71
Potter, Agnes, 213
Pottstown Roamer's Motorcycle Club, 164
Powell Aviate, 205
Prindle, Ruth, 202

Randall, Maud M., 140
Renfrow, Edna, 223
Rice, Dorothy, 13
Rice, Isaac, 13
Riggsby, Lou, 184, 210
Robinson, Betty, 148–151, 225
Robinson, Dot, 15, 130, 148–151, 188, 210, 212, 225
Robinson, Mrs. Henry W., 14
Robinson, Ruth, 143
Rodriguez, Dora, 50
Rogers, Mrs. G. N., 13
Roland, Ruth, 108
Roop, Mabel, 158
Rose, Dorothy, 162–163
Rose, Kathleen, 158
Russell, Jane, 227

Sacramento Cyclettes, 15, 180
San Francisco Motorcycle Club, 34, 36, 60, 158, 181, 206
San Francisco Motorettes, 200
Sargent, Ann, 212
Savannah (Georgia) Motorcycle Club, 52
Scherbyn, Louise, 15, 166–167, 219
Scott, Lizabeth, 228
Sennett, Mack, 120
Sheesley Shows, 132
Shop, Carolyn, 132
Sill, Eleanore, 208
Simms, Virginia, 213
Simplex Servi-Cycle, 214
Sippy, Dorothy, 22
Slaughter, Lillian, 49
Smith, Dot, 165, 206
Smith, H. G., 28
Smith, Helen, 212

Smith, Martha, 212
Smith, Mrs. Roy J., 124
Smith, Pearl Louise, 212
Smith, Ruth, 224
Sonnenfelt, Agnes "Sunny," 216
Stanton, Eleanor, 131
Steiner, Ruth, 229
Steward, Wanda, 209
Stokes, Louise, 213
Stoney Lonesome Motorcycle Club, 217
Strasser, Alena, 213
Stringfield, Bessie, 168
Struck, Gloria Tramontin, 215

Tacoma Motorcycle Club, 190
Talmadge, Norma, 109
Thor, 30, 45
Tassart, Elizabeth, 213
Taylor, Florence, 160, 162–163
Tedjeske, Gwen, 212
Teeter, Irene, 237
Tiger Autobike, 84–85
Travis, Florine, 30
Treadwell, Speedy (Merrill), 133
Triumph, 224
Trumpour, Hazel, 27

Van Buren, Adeline & Augusta, 14, 86–87
Vanderhoof, Mrs. V. M., 14
Varney, Jackie, 221
Vaughan, Helen, 212, 213
Vernon, Dorothy, 106
Vlatkin, Rose, 162–163

Wa-Co-Mo-Pals, 166
Waddell, Minnie E., 51
Wagner, Clara, 22–25
Wagner Ladies' Drop-Frame, 22
Walker, Grace, 92
Walker, Mary, 179
Wall, Mary, 193, 212
Wallach, Theresa, 15
Walters, Easter, 112–113
Waltham (Massachusetts) Motorcycle Club, 14
Wardwell, Sophie, 13, 14, 28
Warren, Bessie, 147
Washington, D.C. Riders, 96
Wells, Claire, 60
Wenbourne, Betty, 13–14, 28
Werner, Florence, 126
Wertz, Mrs. F., 123
Whatley, Ruth, 72
Whipple, Ira H., 26
White, Mary, 67
Wiegand, Mrs. Dona, 160, 162–163
Williams, Mrs. F.H., 28
Williams, Mary, 212
Willingham, Polly, 209
Wills, Pearl E., 49
Wilson, Margaret, 232, 234
Wilson, Mrs. Preston, 175
Winfield, Mrs. E. F., 51
Women in the Wind, 8,
Women's International Motorcycle Association, 8, 166
Woodman, "Cy," 35
Woodson, Scotty, 181

Yale, 27, 52, 55
Yamaha, 8